About James F. Twyman

James F. Twyman is an internationally renowned author and musician who has traveled the world performing The Peace Concert in some of the worst areas of violence and discord. Also known as the Peace Troubadour, he has been invited by government officials and humanitarian organizations to perform in such countries as Iraq, Northern Ireland, Bosnia, Serbia, Kosovo and Mexico, as well as at the United Nations in New York. He has won an international reputation for blending his unique style of music with his talent for drawing millions of people together in prayer to influence the process of peace in countries torn apart by hatred and war.

His ministry began in 1994 when he took the peace prayers from the twelve major religions of the world and arranged them to music. His goal was to show how all spiritual paths point to a single experience of peace. In 1995 he was invited to perform the concert in Croatia and Bosnia during the height of the Balkan war. His best-selling book *Emissary of Light:A Vision of Peace* (Warner Books) recounts his amazing adventures traveling through the mountains of Bosnia and learning the secrets of an ancient society of spiritual masters.

Since 1995 James has helped sponsor several major prayer vigils that have been attended by millions around the world. The most famous was called The Great Experiment, conducted from the United Nations Church Center in New York City on April 23, 1998. More than five million people in at least eighty countries participated in the vigil by attending small prayer circles in hundreds of locations around the world. A month earlier he had been invited by Saddam Hussein to perform The Peace Concert in Baghdad during the same week the US and Britain were preparing to bomb Iraq. A week later James was invited by government officials in Belfast to sing the Prayer of St. Francis at Stormont Castle during the sensitive peace negotiations there.

James F. Twyman received his Bachelors degree from Loyola University in 1984, and a Doctorate in Ministry from Agape Seminary in 1997. He is also the father of a young daughter named Angela.

D0249922

"Open Your Heart"

by Jac Lapointe

*"I open my heart to the emotion that will guide my soul.
In this movement of openness, I release my fears
and cross the threshold leading me towards a new beginning."*

"Our Lady of the Universe"

by Jacqueline Ripstein

Read Part Two of this book to discover
the extraordinary story of this painting.

THE SECRET

of the

BELOVED DISCIPLE

FINDHORN
Press

Also by James F. Twyman

Emissary of Light

THE SECRET

of the

BELOVED DISCIPLE

A community founded by the Apostle John has lived
in seclusion for two thousand years.
The time has finally come for their amazing
secret to be revealed.

By James F. Twyman

Author of the best-selling *Emissary of Light*

First published in 2000

ISBN 1 899171 08 8

British Library Cataloguing-in-Publication Data.
A catalogue record for this book is available from the British Library.

Library of Congress Card Number: 99-67784

Layout by Pam Bochel
Cover design by Thierry Bogliolo
Front cover painting "Open Your Heart" by Jac Lapointe
Back cover painting "Our Lady of the Universe" by Jacqueline Ripstein
Author photograph by Adrian Moore

Printed and bound in the USA

Published by
Findhorn Press

The Park, Findhorn   P.O. Box 13939
Forres IV36 3TY   Tallahassee
Scotland   Florida 32317-3939, USA
Tel 01309 690582   Tel 850 893 2920
Fax 01309 690036   Fax 850 893 3442
             e-mail info@findhornpress.com
             findhornpress.com

Contents

Preface

s we travel through the journey of life, every so often we will meet somebody that is special. This person may be on a mission so profound that we know that they are touching the lives of every one that they come in contact with. Or they may possess a talent that you immediately recognize is a gift from God. When you are in their presence, you feel the essence of their energy, and you are filled with joy.

James Twyman embraces all of these traits.

I first heard of James as a result of his travels to Iraq during the attempted peace negotiations between Saddam Hussein and Kofi Annan, Secretary General of the United Nations. James used his musical talents to perform a peace vigil on Iraqi national television. I recognized then that this man had to be an extraordinarily committed and courageous soul to take on this challenge.

Not too long after, I was introduced to James' first book, *Emissary of Light*. Again, I was fascinated by his commitment to be an agent of peace and love in the world. I was also captivated by the wisdom and drama contained in this true and wonderful story.

During 1998, I had the opportunity to meet James Twyman personally. Both of us had become major speakers around the country for the Whole Life Expo organization. James spoke on the subject of his book, and I participated because I was the subject matter of the best selling book, The Messengers. Now, to me he was no longer James Twyman, but had become my dear friend, Jimmy. He had become a light entering my life. I have attended his workshop and have watched him manifest God's love to his audience in words as well as through his music. Jimmy has the incredible gift of touching the hearts and minds of those he comes in contact with. He's a messenger of God. He is an emissary of love, compassion and hope.

In *The Secret of The Beloved Disciple*, you will travel with the author on a venture that will enhance your own spirituality. You will see and witness life through his eyes. You will travel to places where physically very few people have had the courage to go voluntarily, and you will experience the wisdom and compassion and love manifested by Jimmy Twyman on his incredible journey.

The Secret of The Beloved Disciple reinforces your relationship with the divine and will touch your hearts and souls to their greatest depths. As James shares his personal thoughts and experiences, you also will recognize that you have been taken on an incredible spiritual journey.

Nick Bunick
June 16, 1999

Introduction

t has been said that we are living in a time of prophesy and miracles. Many of the world's ancient civilizations, as well as our own modern religious traditions, have pointed to this moment in history as a time of great spiritual and social transformation. The ancients called this the "time of no time" because they foresaw a great awakening, as if humanity had fallen into a deep sleep and was about to rediscover something marvelous. People from every spiritual path have found themselves suddenly haunted by a memory they thought they had pushed aside — a still, quiet voice that calls them to remember a promise they made long ago. The voice is growing louder, so loud that many people have begun to listen... and change their lives.

In 1993 a female buffalo named Miracle was born in Janesville, Wisconsin. Her owners were amazed at the creature, for she was as white as the snow, but none of them knew just how significant she was. On the same day, hundreds of miles away in South Dakota, a Native American man whose name roughly translates to 'He that Searches for Buffalo', had an amazing dream. He saw a young female white buffalo and the farm she was born on. He also saw the name of the town. When he woke from his dream he believed that he had witnessed the fulfillment of his tribe's most sacred prophesy.

They believed that the world would someday shift away from a masculine society ruled by competition and domination, to a society ruled by the feminine qualities of compassion and love. For hundreds of years they had waited for the signs: a female white buffalo that would be born signifying the birth of a New World. As she grew to adulthood she would change color four times, representing the four races on planet earth. Most important, the father of this young buffalo would die three days after she was born, symbolizing the death of the patriarchy. This ancient prophesy had never been fulfilled, and when the young man and his family left their home in South Dakota to search for the farm he saw in his dream he didn't know what they would find.

They found Miracle when she was only three days old. The family who owned the farm had no idea this young buffalo was the subject of an ancient legend. As far as they knew she was an albino, nothing more. When 'He that Searches for Buffalo' asked to see Miracle's father they explained that he had died earlier of a brain aneurysm. To date Miracle has changed color four times. She is currently red. Native Americans believe that when she returns to her original color, the legend will have been fulfilled. The shift of the ages will suddenly be at hand.

This story and many more show that we are giving birth to a New World. And like a woman who endures the trauma of a difficult labor, there are challenges we must face and obstacles we must overcome. It is reassuring to know that we are not alone on this journey, that we have powerful helpers at our sides. In addition to legends and prophesies like the white buffalo, there are many other stories that tell of angelic interventions, or of spiritual guides who lead us past the obstacles that often block our path, helping us to release ourselves from the chains that have bound us to fear. Many have reported meeting people who appear quite ordinary at first, but prove to be much more.

Are we winding our way toward some pivotal moment in human history, a kind of spiritual quantum leap, and these helpers are making themselves more available than ever before?

In the last several years, dozens of books have reported remarkable first hand encounters with angels and Heavenly beings. In some cases these experiences have crossed that thin invisible line that separates this world from the next, bringing ordinary people face to face with supernatural guides, leading them past the destructive patterns that have chained their lives to fear. These stories are becoming commonplace, as if the doors of Heaven have been opened and we are being showered with celestial light. Nearly every religion admits the existence of angels and their role in helping us transcend the darkened forms that have so dominated our world. It is a sign of the times, another reminder that we are living in one of the most exciting moments in human history. Angels are everywhere, and they're here to lead us into the light.

And yet many others have reported physical encounters with a being that is beyond even the angels. This woman has always been present, guiding us through many of the obstacles we have placed upon our path, barriers that have blocked our experience of the love we long for. Often seen in sacred visions or apparitions, the Mother has acted as a universal way-shower, guiding us through some of our darkest and most desperate nights. And yet there is now an urgency to her message that has not been present before, as if we are suddenly close to the fulfillment of our dreams, or our nightmares, depending upon what we choose. It is her job to assist us in the choices that bring one or the other into tangible form.

Nearly every spiritual tradition acknowledges and honors the feminine, compassionate nature of God. Some identify this being as Tara, Quan Yin, Sofia or Saraswati, but behind them all beats the heart of a mother, a Divine Universal Mother. Christians call her the Blessed Mother, or simply "Mary, the Mother of Jesus." Throughout history hundreds or even thousands of people have reported encounters with this amazing and compassionate benefactor, and yet their experiences have always been filtered through the religious belief systems of their families and culture. With almost all the verifiable apparitions, the message has been the same, an urgent call to humanity drawing our attention away from a constant preoccupation with "self" and toward God and each other.

This is a true story that I believe supports the changing rhythm of our time. Over the last four years I have had experiences I never thought were possible. And all these experiences have led me here, to writing this short book, to sharing what I believe is one of the most important messages of our time. It is the story of how three people responded to an inner call, the call of the Mother, and how it brought them together and inspired them to strive toward what is perhaps the highest ideal we can imagine: to be instruments of peace. I am one of those people, the second is Fr. John, a priest from Los Angeles, and the third is Jacqueline Ripstein, a talented and renowned artist from Mexico.

It is easy now, in retrospect, to see how we were led along different paths, only to merge in the end, like three great rivers that wind along for countless miles before flowing effortlessly into the ocean. That, in fact, is the real message of this book. We all find ourselves walking the solitary path of our own desires and dreams, but in the end we discover that we are One, walking together toward One God. This is what the ancient cultures foresaw, and this is what we see happening all around us, in every country and in every religion.

We are not so far apart after all, and the more we focus on the ways we are the same rather than the ways we are different, the closer we come to reality itself. This has always been Her message, the woman who has come to assist us in our transformation. This story has been told in many ways, by many different people, and yet the essence has always remained the same. We are ready to create the world of our dreams, but only if we are willing to lay aside the separating beliefs that have kept us in darkness.

This book is divided into four sections:

The first section covers my own journey and how I was led to discover the amazing secret of the Order of the Beloved Disciple. It begins in 1994 when I accepted a commission to become the "Peace Troubadour," traveling the world singing peace prayers from the twelve major religions, which I had arranged to music. A year later, while performing throughout former Yugoslavia, I was led to an ancient community of mystics who called themselves the "Emissaries of Light." They said that the time had come for humanity to accept a new vision of peace that would transform the world. They said that someone was coming, for me and for the whole world, and that that person would assist in this global transformation.

Over the next several years I traveled the world performing, teaching and sharing this message, waiting for that "someone" to arrive. I met Fr. John, the eclectic priest who had also dedicated his life to traveling the world promoting peace, and together we left for Serbia armed with nothing but a six-foot pole bearing the phrase, "May Peace Prevail on Earth." Many extraordinary events began to unfold, all culminating in November of 1998 when I saw the painting that changed my life forever.

The second section is the story of Jacqueline Ripstein, the visionary artist who would transfer the message and energy of Our Lady onto a simple painter's canvas. She wondered why she was commissioned by the Church to paint *Our Lady of the Universe*. She wanted a sign, a Divine signal that would show her God's will. The many signs she received were unmistakable, and they inspired her to put her talent to the ultimate test. When the painting was first displayed, hundreds of people were overwhelmed by its transformational power. Priests fell down in prayer in front of the painting, unable to move. Dozens of people began crying uncontrollably, and others reported being able to feel "Our Lady's pulse" when they touched her wrist. It became clear that this was no ordinary painting, and Jacqueline herself would undergo many trials as she accepted her own role as an "instrument of peace."

The third section marks the point these three rivers finally meet. I was asked to write a song that would be used to promote Jacqueline's painting. No one knew that my decision would be the final link the Mother needed to fulfill her purpose. While meditating with the picture on a flight from Denver to San Francisco, I was shown her whole plan — the way she intended to use art and music to bring people into direct communication with the Divine feminine nature of God. A succession of three miraculous phone calls showed me the reality of my "vision," and two days later I performed a concert that changed everything for me.

Finally, the fourth section was written when I thought the book was already finished. The same thing had occurred when I wrote the book *Emissary of Light*. As soon as I thought it was over, as soon as the dust had settled and it seemed I had everything I needed to tell an amazing story with an important, life-changing message, something happened and I would be off to the races again. In this case I found myself drawn to the border of Kosovo and Macedonia at the same time that hundreds of thousands of refugees were trying to escape the ethnic warfare unleashed on them by the Serbian military machine. Everything came together during that trip. All the lessons I had learned and insights I had gained were put to the test and fulfilled in one journey. I realized that the Emissaries were right — we really are ready to create a New World. That is the real message of this book.

It is my goal to express these experiences as accurately as I can. Though this is a true story, certain names and elements were altered to protect the privacy of some of the characters, as well as add to the general rhythm of the story. Everything I have written, then, is either totally true, or is at least based on true events. I encourage you to look within and decide for yourself what you believe is real. I ask only that you "feel" the message of Our Lady, rather than intellectually try to determine its validity. God's voice is heard in the soul, is then experienced by our emotions, and is finally judged by the mind. Therefore, the mind is twice removed from the actual truth.

I admit that much of what you are about to read does not make sense from a physical/perceptual point of view. That's why it's miraculous, for miracles transcend the physical world and bring us a step closer to the Divine. Therefore, just for a little while, let go your judgments and enter into this story with an open mind. Let the Mother reveal herself to you in whatever way she sees fit. Then you will know the truth directly, not because I have said it is so, but because it is within you.

Part One

Complete the triangle," the voice echoed in my mind. It was not the first time I heard those words. The saga had begun when I received the message from Fr. John, the priest from Los Angeles who had accompanied me on my trip to Serbia two years earlier. As soon as I arrived in England I was given the letter he had sent to me through a friend, two scribbled lines that made no sense to me at the time. "Complete the triangle," the words said. "Jesus, Mary and St. John... that's how you'll know it's happening... trust the signs." It was just like him to leave such a cryptic message, and I didn't think much of it at the time. And yet, after I had left Glastonbury on my way to the famous Findhorn community in Scotland, no less than five people had repeated the entreaty.

"Do you know anything about the energy link between Glastonbury, Findhorn and Iona?" Linda asked me. We were taking a break from the Findhorn "Call to Action" peace conference and I had just mentioned my trip to Glastonbury. The small room was filled with people drinking coffee and tea, and I wasn't sure I had heard her correctly.

She leaned forward. "I asked if you have ever heard anything about the..."

"Oh, I understand," I said. "Yes... I think you're the fifth person to mention the connection. What can you tell me about it?"

"I don't know much myself," she said, "only that there are two major ley lines that run through all three towns. When the community of Findhorn was first established, some of the founders knew that all three locations would be energetically linked, creating a powerful vortex. They say that they are all strong feminine energy centers."

"Someone said I should complete the triangle before I go to Kosovo. What do you think about that? Does it make sense?" I was testing her in a way, wanting to see where she would take my question. If she were too sure about her answer then it would lead me to think I was getting some sort of a party line, as if everyone here was told to do the same thing. If she had her own opinion... well, that might be different.

"Only you know if it makes sense," she said. "All I can tell you is that the island of Iona is one of the most powerful places on the planet. In fact, geologists say that it has the oldest rock formation on Earth, two billion years old or something. It's a real mystery. For thousands of years, perhaps beginning with the Druids, there have been goddess cults associated with Iona. It was also one of the first places where Christianity took hold in this part of Europe. St. Columba founded a famous abbey there, and he had great respect for the energy and customs of Iona."

"But what does all this have to do with my trip to Kosovo?" I asked her. "I'm going there to do a peace concert and focus a world-wide prayer vigil. I just don't see the connection between Iona and the suffering that is very real to those people."

"Like I said, only you know if there's a connection or not. If there is, and you want to go check it out, I'll be happy to drive you there. It takes about six hours from here, but you first need to decide if it makes sense."

It did make sense, and I knew it. The first time someone had told me about the Glastonbury/Findhorn/Iona triangle, something moved inside me. Then I remembered the message from Fr. John. It had something to do with the feminine energy Linda mentioned, the divine pulse of the Mother that had haunted me for the last two years... all my life, really. Was she going to show herself to me again, I wondered? My life had not been the same since I remembered my connection to her, and I had the feeling that this trip to Kosovo would complete something. But what? I knew I had to go to Iona, if for no other reason than to gather some strong energy around myself before the difficult journey that lay ahead. Kosovo had exploded in ethnic warfare, and I was about to descend into the middle of the madness. I needed all the help I could get, and Iona sounded like the perfect place to get it.

A day later we were winding our way along the narrow paths that are called roads in that part of Scotland. It was a wonder we made it there alive, or that anyone was able to navigate the sharp turns and one lane roads that hopped from one island to another on the way to Iona. Linda didn't seem to mind the pace, and she was an adept driver. It was the buses that bothered me, the wide tourist type taking up more than their share of the cow-path sized highway. They would appear over hilltops and with sudden abandon claim even the air around our small car. Each time Linda would dart into one of the small turnoffs designed, I imagine, for just such an occasion.

The scenery was breathtaking, all the way from the famed Loch Ness to the high cliffs of the western shore. At times it seemed like a different planet, and then the road would level and a ferry station would appear. We had to take three ferries to get to Iona, the final one being the most memorable. The chopping water of the open sea lapped against the side of the boat, and I could feel the cold chill of the wind that blew me toward something I could not quite grasp. Something was going to happen... something had to happen that would bring closure to one adventure and begin another. Or were they the same, like successive chapters in one long book? I was about to find out which it was. I could feel her calling me... the island, the lady.

Linda had been to Iona before, as had nearly all the residents of faraway Findhorn. It was as if it belonged to them, not in a worldly manner but in a way far more essential. They were grounded there, as if defined by the soil and the waves that beat against the rocks like huge kettledrums. The island had been held sacred long before recorded history, long before the arrival of the Christians, and historians loved to speculate about its mysterious past. There were ruins of convents and monasteries, and Druidic hills from more ancient rituals. The first breath I took as I stepped off the ferry sent a shiver through my whole body. The island was welcoming me, it seemed, blessing me and what I was about to do, the adventure I was about to begin and end. Was this where I would find the door opening to spirit, the Door of Eternity which the Emissaries spoke of?

"I've completed the triangle," I said to Linda.

"Now you have to let the island speak to you," she said with a knowing look. "It's a wonderful, mysterious place, and she knows what you need. I'm going to leave you alone to do whatever you need to do. Let's check into the hotel and you can be off."

The Columba Hotel was a five-minute walk from the ferry, and I could tell that it was something of a nerve center for the island. Linda had called ahead for reservations, and moments after I dropped off my bags I was off and walking. A young Canadian man told me that the strongest energy could be sensed on the opposite side of the island, a half-hour walk, by the cliffs that are said to be the most ancient rock formations on the planet. The sun was dipping close to the horizon and there didn't seem to be much time before it would be gone altogether. I walked as fast as I could along the narrow road, past the ruined nunnery, then up the path that cut to the other side of the island.

Flocks of sheep grazed everywhere I looked, and their endless grazing gave the landscape the appearance of a finely manicured golf course. The gently rolling hills were like waves of green silk that quickened my step, and before long I could hear the ocean again, the rhythmic beating of the tide against the mythic cliffs. The grass suddenly ended and gave way to fine white sand. I crossed that expanse and made my way to the water, then minutes later to the cliffs that hung like a dream above the waves.

I stood there for a moment and gazed at the jagged edges and rough juts of rock. How did they know, I wondered, that these were the most ancient cliffs on planet Earth... the oldest, continuously above water rock formations ever found? What did this fact add to the rich history of the island? I was also told that many of the minerals and rocks that were found on Iona were like nothing else in that area of Scotland. No other island was like it, and this only added to the mystery. Where had it come from, and where would it take me? And how would it prepare me for the trip to Kosovo, the next chapter of my own long history?

I began to climb the cliff and carefully wound my way around to the side that faced the water. When I turned the corner I felt the ocean mist and wind slap against my face. The taste of the salt on my lips was magical, and I reached down and took hold of the dark rocks to steady myself. The wind whistled in my ears and I thought I could hear it calling to me, not by my name but as if it knew me only as a man.

Then I raised my head slightly and realized that someone really was calling me. I saw an old woman sitting on the tiered cliffs above and she was motioning for me to come to her. Her ancient hand waved slightly and her toothless smile seemed to pull me to her like a magnet. I climbed the rocks with little effort, and before I knew it was sitting a few feet to her left.

The woman was even older than she first seemed. Her wrinkles were deep and her clothing was almost ancient. She seemed to be beating her hand on the huge boulder we were sitting on. Then I noticed that she had a small black rock in her hand, and that she was actually tapping the boulder with a slow steady rhythm. There was a slight crack in the boulder about ten inches long in the exact spot where she tapped. I almost had the feeling she had made the crack herself, then dismissed the idea as ridiculous.

"Why are you here?" she asked me. I looked over at her and wondered what I should say. It was a good question, one that I didn't have a good answer for. I came to Iona to complete the triangle, even though I really didn't know what that meant. I came to prepare myself for a peace mission, to travel once again into the heart of despair and war. But why was I there? I smiled and said I wasn't sure.

"You'd better get sure lad," she said with the strongest Scottish accent I had heard till then. "You didn't come here to wander about for nothin'. You're here to live what you were told to live. I know why you're here. I'm very old, older than all this. That means I can see through you, see right to your heart."

"What's your name?" I asked her.

"You can call me 'Old Woman.' I've been here as long as these rocks. I can tell you things that no one else can... things you want to hear."

I looked again at the black rock in her hand. She was still tapping with it on the huge boulder where she sat. She noticed my glance and stopped for a moment.

"It's not how hard you hit something," she said. "It's all about persistence. Even an old woman like me can crack a boulder, not because I'm stronger than you, but because I don't stop. These cliffs you're sitting on have resisted the tide for two billion years. Look how rough and jagged they are. Don't you think you could do the same?"

"I'm not sure I know what you mean." I said these words at the same instant that I realized something very strange was happening. This was not an ordinary old woman I had encountered, and this was certainly not an ordinary conversation we were having. I leaned forward so I wouldn't miss a single word. This is why you're here, I thought to myself. This is the end... and the beginning.

"You've met my daughter," she said as she looked deep into my eyes.

"Your daughter... "

"Yes, you know what I mean. You've met her, and she knows who you are. She's the one who will lead you... lead everyone. I've been here for a long time, but now it's her turn. I've been making the crack in the rock, and she's going to get inside that crack and break it apart. Don't act so stunned. This is what you knew would happen, I just look a little different than you expected."

I did know what she meant, but I couldn't believe it. Was this her, the one that was holding the door open? But it was impossible, nothing at all like I imagined.

"The door is already open," she said. "It has always been open. And I'm too old to keep up this tapping. Here, why don't you keep this."

She tossed me the black rock she was holding and I caught it in my left hand. I felt a wave of confusion rush through me when my fingers closed around it. It was lighter and softer than I thought. It looked like a hard, dense piece of rock, but when I held it in my hand I realized it was wasn't hard at all, more like a solidified piece of volcanic lava. That's exactly what it was — lava. I looked at it, then back at the old woman who was smiling at me again.

"It's a gift from my heart, I guess you could say. By the time my daughter gets done with you, I'll be young again... you'll see. I can't stay this old forever."

"Who are you?" I asked.

"Don't ask questions like that," she said as she stood up and brushed off the back of her rust colored dress. "Just do what you have to do. And remember, there's more at stake than you can imagine. The place where you're going will teach you that. And that's where everything will finally make sense... where you'll understand what my daughter told you."

"You mean Kosovo?" I asked.

"Wherever. The place doesn't matter, or the name, or even you. It's the time that's important, and this is the time. You said something about the door. Well what are you waiting for? You know how to get through... I suggest you get to it."

She turned away and began walking slowly down the cliff toward the ocean. I could hear her mumbling something as she walked, but I wasn't sure if she was speaking the words to me or not. Then she turned around and said, "She'll tell you what you need to know, just like I told her. Just' don't miss it, because it's important. And keep tapping that rock. You'll laugh about it someday... someday when you understand."

Moments later she disappeared around the near side of the cliff and I was suddenly alone again. I looked at the piece of lava I held in my hand, the object of her last remark. What would I understand, I wondered. There were so many things I was confused about, so many unanswered questions from my life. And now this, meeting her on a cliff in Iona. She had shown me so many faces already, so many manifestations of the same reality. But this was different, and what she said was different as well.

I stood up and made my way back to the beach, then to the path that led to the Columba Hotel. The sun was nearly gone and I would have to find my way in near darkness. That didn't seem to matter, for there was now a strong light guiding my path.

The rock was squeezed between my fingers as I walked and I began to recall scenes from the last year of my life, then the last five years. It was all starting to make sense, all the miraculous circumstances that led me on the journey. Then I thought about my childhood, and I wondered if that was where it all began. Maybe there is a thread winding back through our lives that connects everything like an enormous tapestry. If we follow the thread back through the years we learn things that were not so clear to us at the time. Every event makes sense then, and there is a sudden clarity that was lost before.

It was what I had been looking for all along, a way of bringing the loose threads together and finding the hidden pattern. As I walked along the road I recalled the details of the past as I never had before. And for the first time since the adventure began I understood everything.

"It started so long ago," I said to myself, "earlier than I ever expected."

I have always thought of myself as an ordinary person. If anything, I am far too indulgent and self-centered to be an example of spiritual enlightenment, like a saint or a guru who is sought after for sacred attention and advice. I was born with all the "normal" appetites, and I often chased them with ferocity. The most innocuous was my passion for music. Of the five children in my Irish Catholic family I was the one most likely to fall into the wrong crowd, end up homeless and on drugs, or any one of a long list of things my mother feared. It was hard to tell in which direction I would turn, or where my wayward life would lead.

And yet I was also the child most likely to become a priest. This, of course, was my mother's dream. It was the only thing that could save me from certain disaster, she often thought. Some parents pack their children off to the military for discipline. Such a move would have never worked for me since my temperament was directly opposed to such a lifestyle. I would have been thrown out too quickly. But the priesthood, yes, this was different, especially since I had always gravitated toward everything spiritual. I had even conned my way into becoming an altar boy a year ahead of schedule, anything to be close to the smells and bells that so enthralled me. If my parents couldn't save me, perhaps the iron fist of Holy Mother Church could.

Much to everyone's amazement I never resisted this suggestion. In fact, I wanted to begin right away, to enter a high school prep-seminary. This must have confused my parents, since I'm sure they anticipated resistance to their idea. Instead of having to convince me of the merits of religious life they had to slow me down. We decided that I would finish high school, then enter whatever order I chose. My mother braced herself when it came time to make my decision. She, of course, wanted me to stay in Minnesota, away from some big city where I was sure to find trouble. I, on the other hand, had another idea.

I was only eighteen when I joined the Franciscans in Chicago. A month after I graduated high school, I left Minneapolis and moved to Marytown, a large friary in Libertyville, a suburb an hour north of the city. What no one knew was that I had thought about being a priest ever since I began having mystical experiences around the age of twelve. That was how I was raised — if one day you find that God is talking to you, it means you've been 'called'. There were no other options, and that was fine with me. Though I had really only begun to live, I was convinced I knew what I wanted to do with the rest of my life.

Much of my desire to become a Franciscan was based on their devotion to Mary, the Mother of Jesus. Even as a child I was devoted to the rosary, praying all five decades at least once a day for years. I had made a promise to her, sometime around the age of twelve, and though the specifics had receded into the shadows of my consciousness, it haunted me still. I remember kneeling in front of a statue of Mary for hours, praying and weeping, and I felt a wide chasm begin to open in my soul. Something was happening to me, something deep and profound, but I was far too young to know what it was. Perhaps that is why it was happening, because my naïveté made it impossible to judge these things.

Miracles come easily to children, and God's voice is heard so much more clearly during those innocent years. They ask the right questions, simply and directly, and they turn to the earth and to the stars for their answers. Since their minds are open and their spirits undaunted by the savage tyranny of passing dreams, God speaks to them through the elements, and through the wind itself. Someone was talking to me during those early years, and it didn't matter who it was. That soothing voice helped me survive the raging tide of my youth, and like a boat that is fastened to a long rope tied between two shores, I was carried without incident to the other side.

It was that voice I was following when I moved to Marytown. But by the time I was eighteen, it was more like an echo, a fading photograph one carries to remember the details of a face that was once so familiar. The brothers and priests were so much older than I was. Looking back, I know I must have seemed like a baby to them. Brother Pious, who was later to become my mentor and dear friend, was assigned to be my immediate superior. He was to mold and shape me into the perfect friar, or send me packing. The first time we met I sat across from him at his massive old desk. It fit him somehow, for he was as strong and rooted as the wood. But his eyes betrayed him. They were soft and round, and though he tried to test and scare me back into my parent's car, instead I was soothed and reassured by his spirit.

"Do you realize that the average age of the friars here at Marytown is well over fifty?" he asked.

"I didn't realize that, but it doesn't surprise me."

"The days when men enter at your age is over," he said. "I don't really think it's a good idea. You should be in college, doing what normal kids your age do. After that, if you're still interested, you can come back. At least by then you'll have more to go on… you will have lived a little."

"How old were you when you entered?" I asked him.

He smiled slightly. "I was eighteen, true. But things were much different then. Such a choice was very common. It isn't now."

"I know I'm young," I said to him, "but this is what I've always wanted. I believe I've been called here, as if it's been planned somehow. All I ask for is a chance."

"Everyone thinks they've been called," said Brother Pious. "But whether you're mature enough to listen to that call is a different matter. Things won't be easy for you here. You stand the risk of being rejected by the community, not in a malicious way, but because the brothers won't be able to relate to you, and you won't be able to relate to them."

"If what you say is true then I'll leave at that time. But I'm already here, and I feel prepared to make a commitment to this life."

"I will ask you to leave at the first sign of trouble," he said to me. "And you will have to leave without complaint. Is that understood?"

"Yes, Brother."

"I don't want you to suffer or be injured by this experience, James. We will have to see what happens. If Our Lady wants you, then it will all work out."

I felt as if I had passed the first test, overcome the first hurdle in my religious vocation. I would live at Marytown for three months, then move to the House of Studies in Chicago. During the next four years I would work on my Bachelor's degree, then go on for a Master's in Divinity. Somewhere in the middle of all this I would leave for a year and enter the novitiate. It all seemed so romantic to me, like the beginning of a wonderful adventure. And, as it turned out, I was not rejected by the community at all, but fully embraced. I was perhaps an oddity, but within days I was one of them, and everything seemed to be in order. My devotion to the community was deep, and I didn't think I would ever leave.

But then my resolve was tested in a dramatic way. I had entered Marytown with three other men, all older than me. Pat Greenough had already spent a year in a different seminary and years later would go on to be Marytown's Father Superior. He was a funny, likeable man and we became good friends almost immediately. Steve Tippe had moved to Marytown from Milwaukee and adapted easily to the friars' lifestyle. Finally, there was John Paul who took me under his wing the first day I arrived. He was a handsome man in his mid-thirties and we went for long walks around a neighboring lake. It felt good to have an older, seemingly wiser friend who could help me navigate my way through this strange new land. He shared many of his own struggles with me as well, and I felt lucky to have found him.

One evening we were up late talking in the recreation room and John Paul began speaking very intimately about his sexual history. I was so young and naïve and had no way of relating to him, or could see the path he was trying to lead me down. I thought he was trying to deepen our friendship, but I soon realized he had another goal in mind.

He told me how happy he was to have a friend like me at Marytown. Then he said that sometimes men who are very close do intimate things together, things that enhance their relationship. I explained that I wasn't comfortable doing these things, and that I was heterosexual.

"I'm heterosexual as well," he said to me. "Someday when you're older, you'll realize that this is a gift men can share, and it has nothing to do with being gay. It's just a special way of becoming close. I already feel very close to you... I just want to feel closer."

"I've never heard that before," I said. "I don't know if you're right or wrong, but I don't feel comfortable with it."

For the next hour and a half he used his words to back me into a corner. Before I knew it I was considering his logic, and moments later he was touching me. The large room was dark and the other friars had long since retired, and we were alone in the far corner. Even if someone had walked in, it would have been easy to hide what was happening. He touched me and I conjured up erotic thoughts of women, anything to take my mind off the strange reality. Moments later it was over, and he sat back in his chair, a look of satisfaction on his face.

"Maybe someday you'll do the same for me," he said. "But that's enough for one night."

John Paul gave me a hug and said goodnight. I sat there in the dark for a long time sorting through my thoughts, wondering what had just happened. Perhaps he was right, I thought to myself. Maybe I was so naïve that I didn't know about these things, that there were ways of showing love for men of which I was unaware. I went to bed trying to convince myself that there was nothing unusual in what we had done. I fell into a deep sleep and was blessed with comforting dreams.

The next morning I woke up and noticed a strange heaviness in the center of my chest. At 6:30 the friars and candidates would meet in the chapel for the sacred office followed by mass, and I wandered in confused and unsettled. My seat was in the back of the choir, just below the huge statue of Mary to the left of the altar. This is where I would pray for hours a day, giving myself to her, asking her for guidance. Tears would stream down my face as I prayed my rosary, or simply talked to her as if she was really beside me. This particular morning I could hardly look in her direction. I had the feeling that I had done something terribly wrong, and I was afraid that she knew. Halfway through the mass I finally looked at the statue and said a quick prayer.

"Show me what to do," I pleaded. "I don't know what this means, if it was right or wrong. I don't feel happy about what I let him do to me. I didn't even enjoy it. Should I say anything to anyone? Or should I keep it quiet, as if it never happened at all?"

As I looked up at the statue I felt something move inside me. I cannot describe what happened next, but I knew she heard my prayer, and she answered me.

"You didn't do anything wrong," she seemed to say. "But you do need to tell someone. The experience you had did not bring you joy, and was therefore not a holy experience. Love always brings more love, my child. Go and tell Brother Pious what happened, and everything will be fine."

Later that day I asked Brother Pious if I could see him in his office. As I sat down across from him I began to cry. The flood gates opened and I could no longer deny what I felt. Then I told him what had happened the night before. I told him how confused I was and that I was afraid that I had committed a sin. He listened closely and seemed to become visibly angry. But he was not angry at me. He said that he had suspected this already, and that immediate action would be taken. John Paul had gone to Chicago for the day and his things would be boxed up and brought to him. I never saw him again.

We sat together for a long time and Pious helped me understand what had happened. Thanks to him the incident never left a mark, and I was able to grow from it. I never felt any bitterness for John Paul, just a great deal of compassion, considering what he had done to take advantage of me.

"Does this mean you're going to ask me to leave now?" I said.

"What makes you think that?"

"You said that if you notice anyone rejecting me, that I would have to go. I thought that this maybe would apply."

"Listen James, what happened, happened. It was unfortunate, but it doesn't have to change anything. You've been getting along with the other brothers quite well, I think. I for one am not going to let this change anything."

We sat there together for some time talking about a number of things, mainly about how I was getting along with the other friars. That is when I got up enough courage to ask him about a far more intimate subject.

"I have another question I would like to ask," I said to him. "Do you think that God, or Mary, can talk to us? I mean... communicate with us in a real way, with words?"

"I don't see why not," he said. "Church history is full of stories like that. Why are you asking?"

"When I was twelve years old I had a very unusual experience. I was an altar boy and was serving mass when I heard a voice. I couldn't tell if I was hearing the voice with my ears or my heart, but I was sure it wasn't coming from me. The voice was neither masculine nor feminine. And it said fantastic things, about me and about the world. It said that everything is about to change, and that it was time for people to get ready. I had the sense that Jesus was about to come back, and yet that wasn't it at all. It was more that his energy was about to be released, and that people would be able to feel it in new ways. I'm really not sure what it meant.

"And it also said that I was to play a role in whatever was going to happen. All I knew was that it had to do with spreading a message of peace, and that I would travel all over the world. Well, since I was only twelve years old, I didn't know how to respond. My ego took hold of it and I decided that I was 'the chosen one of God.' I went to our pastor and told him that I was in direct communication with God and that it was my role to tell him what he was doing wrong. The church had just removed the kneelers in an attempt to modernize. I told him that God didn't like that decision and wanted him to put them back. My father had to lock me in my room to stop me from going back to the rectory with a new set of demands. It apparently brought a great deal of ridicule."

"How did it all change?" Pious asked.

"I ended up feeling very ashamed and tried to convince myself that it was just my imagination. But I knew it wasn't. Over the years I almost succeeded in putting it out of my mind. Now that I'm here I remember it all, and sometimes I think it still happens."

"You mean you still hear the voice?"

"I wouldn't say it like that," I told him. "I really can't describe it at all. It's more like the voice is all around me, and I suddenly feel the message, as if something is being transmitted to me. Sometimes the whole thing happens in about a second. It's not particularly linear, so it can't be explained."

"I'm just wondering if you're still worried about it," he said, obviously concerned.

"Not at all. I'm not twelve years old anymore, so I'm not misinterpreting it like I did before. It's a wonderful experience when it happens. It makes me feel as if I'm not alone."

"Then I have no problem with it, unless it tells you that we need to remodel the chapel. I can't tell you whether it's real or not. Only you know that. Just remember to judge everything from love. If it makes you feel love, then it's probably from God, regardless of the form."

"That's something Mary told me this morning," I said laughing. It was the first time since I was a child I had told anyone about the voice, and I was happy with his response. It made me feel accepted, and that I wasn't crazy. It also made me feel as if I was in the right place. Marytown was so good for me, I thought. The life of the friars and their devotion to Mary resonated with the deepest part of my being. I vowed at that moment that I would never leave.

But I did leave, and much sooner than anyone expected. I was only with the Franciscans for a year and a half. One day I made my decision, packed my few belongings, and moved from the house of studies into a dormitory at Loyola University. Pious had been right after all. I really was too young and the times were so different than they had been when he was young. The world was different. Thus, for the next three years I became a normal student, pursuing new ideas, testing my maturity, drinking massive amounts of beer, and admittedly smoking more than my share of pot. With the demands of all my new indulgences and my new friends, I was able to forget about the Franciscans, and about Mary.

After I graduated in 1984, I met Linda, a beautiful woman whom I married a year later. Our daughter Angela was soon born and I began adjusting to the life of husband and father. Or at least I thought I was adjusting. Looking back, I realize that it was a role I played, but not convincingly. I was never really suited for the life Linda wanted me to live. She desired a 'normal' husband, and anyone who knew me could attest to the fact that I was anything but normal. The jobs I had never quite worked out, and we were never able to get that house we talked about. It seemed as if we were swimming upstream, against the natural current of the life I knew I was meant to live.

But Linda saw things very differently. This was her life, the family she wanted, and the fact that I never took to it depressed her. She could not understand exactly what was missing or what was wrong. But we were young and even when we tried the best we could, nothing quite 'clicked.' I wanted the river to change, I wanted to adapt and accommodate my family, but once again I failed to find a resting place in the world.

Linda and I split up within two years and I found myself moving from job to job, making just enough money to stay alive. The last remnants of my former life had disappeared and I wandered around in a spiritual desert. The voice I had heard in my youth was gone, silenced by the innumerable layers of thoughtlessness I had piled atop my innocence. The pain of losing my family, and failing at everything I set my mind to, became too much to bear, and, yes, I began to consider the unthinkable. More than anything, I wanted it to end, and there were moments when I actually considered doing it myself.

But I still had my music. It was my refuge, the buoy that kept my spirit afloat during those hard times so shrouded in darkness and despair. Music was the one thing I could do better than most everyone I knew, and it never deserted me from the moment I began learning to play the guitar at the age of twelve. I went on playing, and before long I had begun writing music. The songs were simple and crude, but they sparked me in a way that nothing else could. I had rotated constantly between wanting to be a rock star and my desire to follow the 'call', as I referred to it then. The thought that there could be a way to combine these two loves never occurred to me, for I believed that one was 'of the world' and the other was far removed from it.

Years went by, and my life wound its way through a labyrinth of varied circumstances. Months would sometimes pass when I didn't even pick up my guitar. Then something would happen, either in my external or my internal world, and the music would draw me back, like a thin glowing thread that had been left to lead me out of a dark cave. The music would return, and my voice would lift above the din and rediscover the rich pastures of my youth, those deeper moments when I could see further than before. The waters became calm and the wind would subside, and suddenly everything made sense again.

In 1990 I discovered an amazing secret. How could I have known that my constant preoccupation with the dramatic failure of my life was actually fueling my continued failure? Humans seem to have a natural drive to dig bravely into the pit of their desperate circumstances, thinking that they can pull themselves free through sheer will. We've been taught that asking for help is a sign of weakness, and that surrender is the same as failure.

In truth, real growth does not begin until we do ask for help, when we admit that we cannot pull ourselves from the hole we have dug. And the help we are offered has but one lesson: "Give that which you need." *The Prayer of St. Francis* immediately springs to mind: "For it is in giving that we receive, and in pardoning that we are pardoned." It became painfully obvious that I didn't have the answer, for myself or for anyone else. "Begin there," I heard a voice say to me. "If you want love so desperately, then give love. If it's peace you lack, then offer it to another."

The voice had returned, though I didn't comprehend what was happening. Whether it was conscious or not, I found myself gravitating toward its counsel. A friend introduced me to St. Catherine's Catholic Worker in Chicago, a community of six volunteers who worked full time with homeless men and women living with AIDS in one of the city's poorest neighborhoods. One day I went for a visit and the next day I moved in.

For the next two years I lived more of a Franciscan lifestyle than was ever possible with the friars. The joke I often told was that I never lived better than when I was a Franciscan, a strange contradiction. We had nuns cooking for us, doing our laundry, and the house of studies where I lived while attending Loyola University was far from austere. Life was very different at St. Catherine's. Most of our food was donated, and the few dollars we used to run the house trickled in from a handful of patrons who believed in what we were doing. Within weeks I forgot about myself and began focusing on the needs of others. And like a miracle, my problems seemed to vanish.

I look back at those months as some of the best of my life. I learned more about homelessness, drug abuse and AIDS than I ever expected. The faces of those we served are still etched in my mind. When I left two years later I was a different man, living with different priorities and goals. The voice had been right; I had given what I needed most — love. And the love that returned transformed my life.

By 1994 I was living in Wisconsin with a group of friends studying *A Course in Miracles,* the book that changed my life. I was 32 and could finally see past many of the dark forms that had so dominated my life till then. I was regaining my spiritual focus, like a fire that fades and dims, only to be reborn with the sudden change of air. My music stretched in concert with my soul, as if they were the same thing, as if they both expressed the same longing for the innocence I had lost. Thus, it was only a matter of time before I began arranging prayers to music, the prayers that moved and overcame me. It was a kind of balance, the marriage of art and spirit, the devotion of the past and a promise for the future.

One day a friend gave me a sheet of paper on which were written the peace prayers from the twelve major religions of the world. I picked up the sheet as I sat alone in my room and began to read. The Hindu Peace Prayer was first on the list:

"Oh God, lead us from the unreal to the real.
Oh God, lead us from darkness to light.
Oh God, lead us from death to immortality.
Shanti, shanti, shanti unto all."

As I read the prayer I began to sense something amazing. I could hear music, as if someone was playing an instrument in the next room. Then I realized that I wasn't hearing the music with my ears, but with my heart. It was the *prayer*. The prayer was singing itself to me. I picked up my guitar and played along. The music was beautiful, and it continued until I finished the entire song. Then I began reading the Buddhist Prayer for Peace and the exact experience repeated itself. One by one, I read the prayers and played the music. Not one of them took more than five minutes, and when it was over I realized I had just received an amazing gift. I also knew that one is never given a gift of this magnitude unless one is meant to share it.

There are times in all our lives when the tumblers of circumstance fall into place and a door suddenly opens on which we had previously battered in vain. All those past experiences, living at St. Catherine's and studying *A Course In Miracles,* they all prepared me for that perfect moment when Heaven opened its gates and sang its prayer of peace to my open soul. And like the ground fully parched from lack of rain, I drank in that light and let it soak me. I had waited, though not patiently, for this sudden dawn, and I would not let it pass till we were joined. The music and the prayers wed themselves, and I was but their witness.

Within months I was traveling all over North America performing "The Peace Concert." I wanted to show that all the major religions of the world pointed in the same direction — towards Peace. Beyond the rituals and dogma that seem to separate us from one another is an experience that binds us together and makes us one. We all want the same thing, for ourselves and for those we love. This is the one thing we can agree upon, no matter where we live or what religion we practice. Peace is the key, for our inner sanity and that of the world. It is more than a path to unity, it is the very essence of the goal.

I can remember concerts where three people showed up. The information I sent out called me a "penniless, homeless, mendicant troubadour singing for peace." This didn't seem to help; it just raised more questions like, "What's a mendicant?"

"It's a word that used to refer to St. Francis," I would say. "It means that you've left the world behind, at least the desire to make money and get rich. You've chosen a higher path, given yourself to God... left everything."

"But why do you have to be homeless?" they often asked. "Can't you do the same thing and still live a normal life?"

I always hated this discussion. It was as if an ancient monk would suddenly possess my body, a strange residual from the months I had spent with the friars emulating their sacred lifestyle. I truly believed that I had to be poor in order to serve God. How could you have money and be loved by God? But for me it was a subtle escape mechanism, because it meant that I didn't need to be responsive to the pressures that had so overwhelmed me during my marriage. Claiming the ideal of 'voluntary poverty' was my way of dropping out, of not facing the fears that had ruined my relationship with Linda, and the idea kept me running away from life itself.

At the same time something profound had suddenly congealed within me. I may have been running away from society, but I was running toward my destiny. Performing "The Peace Concert" cemented and allied the two most important forces in my life — my music and my spirituality. In one afternoon, the day I received the amazing gift of the peace prayers, they became one and the same. It was clear that I was being used; even my weaknesses were being taken advantage of and employed by God. Oh, what a strange and wonderful thing it is to be used in this way. What a rare gift I was being given, though I was hardly in a position to know it at the time. Pieces of the puzzle were still missing.

In the summer of 1995, long before I went to Iona, I received an invitation to bring "The Peace Concert" to former Yugoslavia, which had erupted in a devastating ethnic war four years earlier. By then I was being called the "Peace Troubadour," but the idea of performing in war zones did not initially appeal to me. I knew very little about the situation, only what I had seen and heard on the evening news. It looked frightening and out of control. How was I going to make a difference, an American musician who had no real concept of war? It was hard for me to accept the direction in which I seemed to be moving, but the miracle that began when I read those twelve prayers had suddenly jumped to an exciting new level, and there was nothing I could do about it.

I was performing for the international Pax Christi conference in Assisi, Italy, just before I was to leave for Croatia, when the spirit of that one-time home of St. Francis began to work its magic on me. One of the things

I learned during that trip, much to my amazement, was that I was not St. Francis. I was nothing like him, and I didn't want to be, nor did I have to be. I was suddenly filled with a sense of my own purpose, not that of another. There was something happening, something important, but I didn't know what it was.

Was it just my imagination, drawing on the strange wanderings that had dominated my youth, the years I had spent dreaming of the "important and critical" role I would play in the history of the world? They were the childish dreams of one searching for attention, not true understanding. But, no, it was nothing like that... more of a subtle knowing, the faint scent of an encounter that would change everything. How could I have known how close it was?

When the bus finally arrived at Rijeka in Croatia, I snatched my guitar from the overhead bin and stood up to leave. I could feel the tension mounting as soon as we crossed the border between Croatia and Slovenia. It felt like a dull pain you want to forget but which dominates every thought. The answers to the questions I asked about the war, about the bloody fight for independence from Serbia, or the long history of violence and hatred, all gave me a one-sided view, depending, of course, on whom I surveyed. That made me feel uneasy. Why had I accepted the invitation to come to this savage place? What good was I going to do, an American who didn't have the slightest idea what was going on? The music and prayers I bore were my only weapons, and I wondered if they were strong enough. The Peace Troubadour was about to have his first test, and I had a terrible feeling that I wasn't ready for it.

Three women, however, made my transition bearable and helped me understand the real reason I was invited to this violent place. I met Snjezana and Gordana the moment I left the bus at the Rijeka station. They were both from Suncokret, the peace organization that had sponsored my trip. Then there was Nadina, the young woman who taught me the personal side of this raging conflict. She was a Bosnian refugee who volunteered at Suncokret, talking depressed young Croatians and Bosnians out of committing suicide. It was good therapy for her, I'm sure, since her own life was as uncertain as anyone she was trying to help.

I spent long days and nights with these friends, and through them I learned what it meant to live in a country at war, a civil war, which is the worst kind. Friends and neighbors turn on each other in a manner that is impossible to imagine. Nadina, a Muslim by birth, was from a small city in Bosnia that was marginally dominated by the Bosnian Serbs. Generations earlier, the Serbs, devout patrons of Eastern Orthodoxy, spread into various parts of Bosnia to live amongst their Muslim neighbors. And though this partnership was often successful, at least on the surface, there was a river of resentment beneath the smooth, impenetrable surface of their consciousness that went back centuries. The Serbs felt that the Muslims were still the sell-outs who had buckled beneath Turkish tyranny hundreds of years earlier, and the hatred that resulted would be visited upon each successive generation. It lurked in the dark corners of their collective unconscious, waiting for the right moment, the opening that hatred needs to spring forward and consume everything in its sight.

The death of Tito provided the perfect opportunity, the first link in a chain of circumstances that suddenly and violently unlocked the dark chambers where their hatred had been sent to seethe. First Slovenia declared independence, then Croatia, and the war that followed became the most shocking European conflict in fifty years. But it was just a warm-up for the horrifying rampage that was soon to follow. The cultural weave that defined Bosnia was too much to tolerate, at least from a Serbian perspective, and it had to be broken. While the Muslims waited for help from NATO and its allies, they were slaughtered. Entire towns were wiped clean, or 'cleansed'. Hundreds of years of animosity finally found its stage, and the performance was catastrophic.

Nadina told me about the day her Serbian neighbor showed up at the door. They had known each other since childhood, and a harsh word had never passed between them. But the opportunity to vent his anger was too much for him, and he seized it with vigor.

"You have twenty-four hours to leave this house and this town," he said with a gun in his hand. "This house now belongs to me and my family. If you are not gone by the time I return, I will put a bullet in your head, and then I will rape your mother."

The attack of his words was just as devastating as the savagery he promised, and Nadina nearly collapsed at the door. But somehow she held herself straight and did not show her fear. She didn't want to give him that pleasure, the satisfaction of watching her cower before his brutal use of inhuman force. Hours later, Nadina and her family joined hundreds of others who had received the same ultimatum, walking in a line to an uncertain future. They left their town, their country and their lives, before finally ending up in Rijeka.

Snjezana and Gordana were luckier than Nadina, but they were not isolated completely. Born and bred in Rijeka, they were not subject to the horrors common to many others in their fractured homeland. It was a fact of geography, really, the result of being so close to Italy. To attack Rijeka was to risk involving the rest of Europe, and that was a gamble that even the unsparing Serbs did not want to take. Their borders were already crippled and their allies few, so it was best to keep the war close to home, and that made Bosnia perfect.

Suncokret served the constant flow of refugees who rushed into Rijeka with the speed and force of a tornado. Snjezana and Gordana worked primarily with women and families to help them secure the basics of life, the food and shelter they would need to survive, and Nadina, as mentioned before, spent hours each day sitting next to the crisis phone waiting for the lonely and distressed to call. Within days I felt an unexpected bond with these women, and a firm respect for the way they rose above each discouraging day.

It was Gordana who had arranged for my invitation. She had read the letter I had sent weeks earlier, the letter saying I would be in Europe and wanted to sing the peace prayers there. She told me that she had felt something strange when she read those words, as if the circumstances surrounding the war and Suncokret and my concert suddenly converged, showing her what needed to be done. But why? Neither of us had an answer to that question, only the deep sense that something profound was taking place, like the plot of a movie winding its way to the climax, unaltered and unobscured.

I performed the concert in Croatia many times, on television, radio and on stage. And though it seemed I was doing exactly what I had been invited to do, I felt there was something missing. From the moment I arrived I sensed that there was another reason why I was there, but I didn't know what it was. Then I began to hear rumors of a secret society of mystics who were said to live somewhere in the mountains along the borders of Croatia and Bosnia. And yet no one seemed to know if there was any truth to these rumors. I decided it was a local myth and tried to forget the whole idea. But fortunately, the idea didn't forget me.

At night there were dreams that told me more than the rumors I heard during the day. Each night I found myself in a domed building, talking to a group of people whom I seemed to know, but when I woke up in the morning the dream would fade, and I found myself back where I began. There was one face I couldn't forget though, that of an old man who seemed to know everything about me. Words and phrases would return to me during the day, and I would see his face as if it were real. But who *were* these people and where was I going at night? There were moments when I couldn't tell the difference between the waking and dreaming worlds, one with wars and refugees, the other filled with light. I began to believe there was a connection between my dreams and the rumors I was hearing about the community in the mountains. But how could I know for sure?

I soon learned that the place in my dreams was not a rumor at all. I met a man named Duro who told me he was the liaison between the world and the community which he called the "Emissaries of Light." He said that he was instructed to bring me to the Emissaries because they had a special message they wanted to give to the world. They had been praying in these mountains for many years, the man said, and yet their role was about to come to an end. People were nearly ready to step into the actual experience of peace, not just the idea or intellectual concept. It was time for humanity to open up to a new level of spirit, one that involved direct contact with the Divine. If I would allow him to lead me to these masters, they would show me how to use prayer to change the world. It was my choice.

Was this where the music and prayers were meant to lead me? I began to see a pattern, and yet there was no way to trace its path and discover the source. Had it begun the moment I heard the song, when the prayers effortlessly arranged themselves to music? Or was it long before that day, planting its seed in the desperate soil of my aimlessness? I could feel the seed pushing up from the soil and trying to breathe. No longer would it sleep beneath the dirt, but stretch toward the sky and seek lighter air.

Nothing could have prepared me for what Duro said. The dreams and feelings from the previous few days fell to the ground like a lead weight, and I was ready to leave everything behind — my friends, the concert, and my so-called destiny. It was a crazy idea, like Shangri-La in the middle of a war zone. The region Duro described was controlled by the Bosnian-Serb army. This was not a hike in the woods he was suggesting, but a flirt with death. Even if everything he said about this community of spiritual masters was true, and I was hardly sure of that, I would have to be insane to follow him.

And yet I would be lying if I said that I wasn't intrigued. As far-fetched as it all was, there was something about his story that I had to trust. It was the only way to explain the dreams and the strange feelings that began when I arrived in Croatia. I looked back at my life, everything that brought me to that moment — the mystical experiences I had had as a child, the Franciscans, all leading up to the wonderful way I received the music that accompanied the twelve peace prayers. Each one was a pearl on a chain that led me to the moment when I would decide whether to get on a bus and return to Italy, or go to the Emissaries. I thought about Pious and the trust he once had in me. He seemed to know that something like this would happen someday. What was I going to say? Would I follow Duro, or turn and leave?

I said yes to my destiny. We left the next morning and began a trek into the mountains of former Yugoslavia to find thirteen people meditating for peace in a domed building. It was a dangerous journey, like an ancient pilgrimage to a sacred and holy place where one encounters the darkest and most dangerous of all adversaries — one's own fear. Duro led me between the troops and away from possible discovery until we finally arrived at a lonely village far from the eyes of the world. In the center of this place stood a building I knew all too well, a large and radiant pagoda with a domed roof. We had arrived; I wondered if I would ever want to leave.

For the next twelve days I lived with the Emissaries high in the mountains of Bosnia. Just as Duro had said, the Emissaries claimed to have been praying for humanity to take the next step in our spiritual evolution, a step away from fear and into love. Seven men and six women came together in the domed building every night at midnight, then sat down at their predesignated spot around a twelve-spoked wheel drawn on the floor. For the next twelve hours they sat motionless, deep in meditation. To observe with physical eyes alone would reveal nothing, but the energy I felt issuing from that geometric form was astounding.

I cannot explain what that means, for I still do not understand it myself. I was allowed to attend each of the meditations during my visit, but to this day I do not fully appreciate the significance of their vigil. I can, however, attest to what I felt in their presence. It was as if a fountain of holiness showered from that sacred place in the mountains, falling over the whole world like a gentle and refreshing rain. That rain would remind us of who we are, the essence of truth which we seem to have forgotten. And they would continue this ritual, just as they had for hundreds or perhaps thousands of years, until the day came when they would no longer be needed, when there would be enough people in the world giving that same light to everyone they met.

"That time is now," he said to me. It was the man I had seen in my dreams, the old master who sat at the center of the wheel, the focal point of the community, the one whom I called 'Teacher.' I met him in his tiny hut in the forest every afternoon where he patiently explained the deeper truths that had eluded me for so long, the message which the Emissaries wanted the whole world to hear.

"Everyone is feeling the change," he said to me, "the great shift that has been prophesied by many of the ancient cultures and civilizations. The Emissaries have existed in the secret places of the world preparing humanity for this moment, preparing them from the inside out you might say. That's why we live in seclusion, in a country where hatred seems to have conquered love. The dense energy in a place like Bosnia actually amplifies the work we do, like a powerful spot light turned toward the darkest of places. Our work ends when people begin to turn their eyes toward love and away from the darkness that has ruled the world for so long."

"But why do you believe we are approaching that time?" I asked him. "Things are worse than they've ever been, at least in some ways. There is more crime and more drugs and anger... "

"But there is also more love and compassion than the world has ever seen," he said. "Both are true. Think of the world as if it's a rubber band. One hand is pulling it in one direction, and the other hand pulls it in the opposite direction. The tension increases until what happens?"

"It breaks."

"Exactly. The tension of the rubber band is greatest the instant before it snaps. And when it breaks, whatever it was holding together falls apart. Do you understand what I am saying?"

"Not really."

"The reality you perceive, the world you see all around you, is based on one single concept — that you are separate from everything. You have a body that seems to separate you from other bodies, and you have thoughts that are different from other thoughts. Do you understand? That is what the rubber band is holding together, the thought system that is based on separation. What I'm saying is that such a perception was never true. It has always been just an illusion that had no foundation in reality. When the rubber band breaks, or when the concept of separation ends, then you'll experience the truth that lies behind this lie — the law of unity. You are one with everyone and everything, so the shift I'm speaking of, the awakening which the prophets foresaw hundreds or thousands of years ago, is really the shift into what is true, into reality itself."

"But what about all the suffering in the world?" I asked. "Are we supposed to close our eyes and pretend it doesn't exist?"

"Your eyes are already closed," he said. "I expect you to open them and solve your problems in a new way. The world seems to present an endless number of problems to solve. You focus on one and three others creep up on you. If you realized that the solution to all your problems is already within your grasp, then you would be able to change the world in an instant. You believe it will take years or lifetimes to solve things like hunger, disease and violence. That's because you keep looking for an answer outside yourself. The answer is within you, a simple readjustment to the way you perceive everything. Change your perception and the world itself will change."

"It all sounds too simple," I said to him. "There must be more to it than that."

"Why? Is it possible that it is simple, and that your need to see it as complicated has been the very thing that has kept you from the answer? What if *you* are the answer? What if it has nothing to do with changing anyone else, but rather that the problem and the solution are intimately linked to your mind?"

"But what about everyone else?" I asked.

"Forget about everyone else. What if there isn't anyone else out there? What if your decision is the only one that matters?"

"I don't understand what you mean."

"A great mystic once said that trying to teach other people about enlightenment is like being in a dream and saying you're not going to wake up until everyone in your dream wakes up. You're going to be there for a very long time with that attitude. What I'm trying to get you to see is that your decision affects everyone's decision, simply because you are everyone."

I began to wonder if I would ever understand him. His lessons were so far removed from my experience, so far beyond my logical mind, that it seemed impossible. Either he was completely wrong, or everything I had ever learned from the world was an illusion. It was hard to tell which it was since the Emissaries obviously possessed powerful abilities that astounded me. Their ability to read thoughts and psychically control their environment was amazing. It gave me more than enough reason to seriously consider what I heard, for they certainly knew something I didn't.

Duro had told me that the Emissaries had a message they wanted the world to hear. That, it turned out, was the real reason I was brought to former Yugoslavia, not to sing and perform the Peace Concert, but to receive that message, then carry it from the secret retreat in the mountains to the rest of the world. During the twelve days I spent with them, I began to experience the rhythm and pulse of the "Emissary message." Their lives emanated the truths they expressed to me, as well as the shift they believed was transforming the planet.

"The main thing you will tell people is that they're ready for what is about to happen," he said to me. "Many will be fooled by the simplicity of this message, but remember — the deepest truths are always clothed in the humblest garments. There is nothing complex about what is to happen. It is in fact the most natural thing you can imagine, like a child entering puberty, or an adolescent becoming an adult. There will always be pains, adjustments and challenges, but that doesn't mean they should be avoided or feared. A child cannot stunt his or her growth because they are afraid of the natural transitions of life. It will occur with or without the child's consent. But their experience of their new life can be perceived in one way or another: it can be a happy change or one that is traumatic. That is the only choice. Growth will occur on its own."

"Are we entering adolescence or adulthood?" I asked.

"It depends upon your point of view. In many ways we have been behaving like children and it's time to grow up. The shift could mean taking responsibility for our actions and the ways we have abused each other and the planet, the same type of adjustments one makes when one becomes a teenager. But humanity has also made incredible leaps in consciousness. Many are ready to experience what it means to be spiritually mature, and those people will help nurture the others. We are really like a family with many siblings at different levels of growth. And yet we are the same, one unit working together and learning what it means to be alive."

"So what is the message you want the world to hear?" I asked.

"There are two simple truths people need to accept if they are to move effortlessly into the New World, the world which is based on the laws of love. You will tell people these truths in whatever way you choose. There are many that have chosen to take the important step of becoming the 'New Emissaries,' and these people will understand. They are the ones you are being sent to help, and they will not misinterpret the simplicity of the message, but will be enlivened by it."

And then Teacher told me the Emissary message, the two simple truths that changed my life. In the last three years I have traveled around the world expressing these truths in any way I can. They have changed the lives of many, simply because we're finally ready to hear them.

"The first message can be said in two words — *You're Ready*. You are ready to release the fearful beliefs that have kept you bound to the concept of separation. You are ready to accept the reality of love that is the foundation of your existence. And you are ready to give love to everyone in every way, for that is the only way you will fully experience it for yourself. These two words, so easily overlooked, are the catalyst that triggers your experience of a New World, a world where hatred and war are forgotten, and peace is the only law.

"The second message can be said in only three words — *You Are Holy*. Who you really are, the essence that God perceives, is beyond the scope of your imagination. If you are one with the Divine Pulse of creation, then you are also one with the holiness of God. That cannot change, simply because God cannot change. When you realize this, when you begin to perceive this truth within everyone you meet, including yourself, then the world will change by itself. You will watch the miracle of love unfold before your eyes, simply because you have affirmed what is true, that you are one with God, and therefore with everyone. You are holy, and that cannot change. Rejoice in that knowledge, for it is the foundation of the New World, the world you are about to enter."

Then he said something I will never forget, words that haunted my memory for the next three years.

"And when you accept these messages, that you are ready, and that the truth in you is the very essence of holiness, then you will recognize the next teacher — the Messenger of Love. It is this teacher who will take you through the *Door of Eternity*, to the very seat of the soul. When you and others have opened your heart to this experience, then humanity will enter a new era, one that is ruled by compassion and grace. At that time you will understand everything, not with your mind but with your heart."

"What is the *Door of Eternity?*" I asked.

"It is a doorway to the real world, a bridge that connects this world with your true home, what you would call Heaven. It has always been right in front of you, waiting for you to enter. But you have been convinced that you must die to enter, as if your body is the barrier keeping you from the joy God would give you. The only barrier blocking your entry is your fear. When you release the fearful patterns that have ruled your life and accept the love that binds you to the Divine, then Heaven will sweep you up like a mother does her child. You are like the child that stands crying because it believes it wants to be alone. It is your mother's arms you seek, not loneliness. In your arrogance you have denied the love that would set you free. And yet that love has never left you, waiting for the moment when you would open your eyes and accept it."

"How do I enter that door?"

"I cannot tell you. The next teacher will explain everything. You will have to go through many trials before that one comes to you, but when you are ready, when humanity itself is ready, the Door will open and Heaven will have it's way."

Many extraordinary things happened during my days with the Emissaries of Light, but the words I heard from Teacher that particular day changed everything. I knew that I would devote my life to sharing their message, but I couldn't have guessed what lay ahead, all the adventures and challenges. There I was, at the very heart of a war I didn't understand, an ethnic conflict that seemed to contradict everything the Emissaries were telling me. There were still so many questions, and yet something tremendous happened to me in the mountains of Bosnia, and all I wanted to do was share it.

The book *Emissary of Light* was published a year later. I began traveling around the world telling people the two simple truths the Emissaries had shared with me. Before long I found myself being invited to more countries experiencing extreme violence, and the *Peace Concert* began to have an incredible impact on international politics. Saddam Hussein, the beleaguered president of Iraq, asked me to perform the *Peace Concert* in Baghdad the same week that another war seemed inevitable. Days later I received an invitation from a government official in Northern Ireland to sing at Stormont Castle in Belfast during the peace talks there. Concerts in Jerusalem, Mexico, and the United Nations also proved that there was something incredible happening to us all. Each time I performed, millions of people would gather around the world in small groups, in churches, in their homes, and even through the Internet, to pray for peace. And each time a powerful pulse echoed through the world, calling humanity to awaken the spirit of compassion and forgiveness.

But there was one question I kept asking myself: Who is the 'next teacher' whom Teacher spoke of... the 'Messenger of Love'? He said that this teacher would symbolize the shift in consciousness from fear to compassion, and I began to sense that this teacher was not for me alone, but for the whole world. Impatience tugged at my heart. When would I meet the one who would take me through the 'Door'?

n March of 1997, I received a letter from a man named Risto Rundo inviting me to perform the Peace Concert in Belgrade, the capital of Serbia. The peace accord ending the war in Bosnia had been signed a year earlier, but tension was still extremely high. At the time, tens of thousands of demonstrators were taking to the streets every day in Belgrade to protest their president's tyrannical policies. The invitation challenged me to proceed with the mission to which I had dedicated my life — continuing to serve as the Peace Troubadour. "We need this concert," he said to me in the letter. "We have such a strong desire for peace."

Around the same time an unidentified person sent me a newsletter that highlighted an article called, "The Zagreb Mandala." It said that there were a number of young people in Croatia and Slovenia who had had a vision of a twelve spoked wheel. The vision, it turned out, was so profound that they drew out the wheel on the floor and used it as the focus of their meditation. When I looked at the published drawing I was amazed. It was almost identical to the Emissary wheel I had seen in the mountains of Bosnia, the wheel that was the center of their mystical meditations. There had to be a connection between these people and the Emissaries I had encountered, and since I would soon be leaving for Belgrade I decided it was the perfect opportunity to find out just what it was.

I called the publishers of the newsletter and told them my story. Then I asked them for a phone number in Croatia. "You don't need to wait to see them in Croatia if you don't want to," the woman said. "Two of the main people from the group, Ishtar and Maya, are in Southern California... San Diego I think. You can contact them there if you want."

The fact that I was making the call from Los Angeles made my choice decidedly easy. I called the number I was given and spoke first to Maya, and after a few moments we decided to meet. I then told her about the Emissaries, wondering if my story made sense to her. There was a long pause on the other end when I finished.

"Come as soon as you can," she said to me. "It is very important that we speak... in fact it is urgent."

I drove to San Diego the next day with my friend Jennifer. The two-hour drive helped me air many of the thoughts swirling through my mind, the confused disjointed wanderings that had dominated the year and a half since I first met the Emissaries. Maybe this is the beginning of the next phase, I thought to myself. Maybe they know who the 'next teacher' is.

"Don't you think the 'next teacher' will come when you're ready?" Jennifer said. "The more you think about it, the longer it's going to take if you ask me. Just relax and do what the Emissaries said to do. The book is out and people are getting the message. That's why you were brought there in the first place. When the time is right, it will happen."

"I can't stop thinking about it," I told her. "There was something about the way Teacher described the 'next teacher' that seemed so urgent. I'm glad the book is out and I'm happy the Emissary message is being heard, but this is the next step for me. I feel like I'm at a standstill until the 'next teacher' appears."

"That's exactly what I'm saying. You're at a standstill because you want to be. You've been given an incredible job, traveling around the world extending everything you learned from the Emissaries. If you keep focusing on what you think is going to happen in the future, you're going to miss what's happening right in front of you."

When we arrived at the apartment complex where Maya and Ishtar were staying, I felt a strange unsettled feeling in my stomach. We stood next to the car for a moment and I wondered about what was happening to me.

"What's the matter?" Jennifer asked.

"I'm not sure. As soon as we pulled up I felt something tugging at my solar plexus. It feels as if I'm not supposed to be here for some reason."

"We drove two hours to get here," she said. "What good is it going to do us if we turn around now?"

She was right. I had no idea what the feeling meant, or if it meant anything at all. Maya and Ishtar could be the connection that leads me to the 'next teacher,' I thought to myself. There was no way I was going to turn back.

We knocked on the door and heard the bolt slip as it unlocked. Maya opened it smiling, her long blonde hair still wet from the shower.

"I'm sorry, but I just finished getting dressed," she said. "Please come in. Ishtar will be ready in a few moments."

She led us to a small room with three chairs, the living room as far as I could tell. We sat down and Maya disappeared into the kitchen.

"Would you like some tea?" she asked. I looked over at Jennifer and she shook her head.

"No thank you," I said to her. "We're both fine. By the way, how long have you been in San Diego?"

Maya came back into the room and sat down across from me. She looked so young, younger than even her nineteen years. And yet her eyes told me more, the sort of eyes one acquires through pain and sorrow. They were tired and dark, as if they needed a long rest. Otherwise she looked no different than any other teenager, regardless of where she was from.

"We have been here for only one week," she said as she sipped from a cup of tea. "We have been in Southern California for nearly a month, but we will wait for Ishtar before we tell you our story."

Just then a tall thin man with deep, penetrating eyes stepped out of the bedroom. Jennifer and I stood to shake his hand.

"I am Ishtar," he said, then sat down next to Maya.

"Now that we are all here we can begin," Maya said. "From what you told me on the phone it seems we have a great deal in common. Ishtar is the one who had the vision of the wheel. It is because of him that several of us came together to meditate for peace. But that is only one of the reasons we sit around the wheel. We believe that it is time for us to ascend, and we need to find our ascension family here on earth. We each had a dream of a community of spiritual masters who live somewhere in Southern California, somewhere in the hills we believe, and we know that these are the people we must find. They are ready to ascend and we are meant to go with them."

As Maya talked Ishtar looked at me, as if his eyes were laser beams that would cut through my consciousness. He never said a word, but watched Jennifer and me with an unwavering stare.

"In our dream," Maya continued, "the dream we had together the same night, we saw a house that we believe is in Pacific Palisades. The people who live in that house will know of this community, and they will lead us there."

"What do you believe will happen then?" I asked.

"We will ascend," Ishtar finally spoke with a dark tone in his voice. "That is why we have come here, and we must find them."

"We have called several hundred people looking for that house," Maya said as she put her hand on Ishtar's. "Each person gave us a few more names and we asked them all the same question. We described the house we saw in our dream and asked them if they knew where it was. Everyday we walk through the neighborhoods of Pacific Palisades looking, but we have not found it yet. We have no money, and until recently we slept wherever we could. We are here in San Diego visiting a friend we know from home. In a week we will go back to LA and continue our search."

"Where will you stay?" Jennifer asked her.

"Two weeks ago we met a priest named Fr. John and he took us into his home," Maya said. "He has been to Croatia and Bosnia several times doing the same kind of work you do, Jimmy. I believe you should meet him. It may be important for both of you."

I looked over at Jennifer and sensed that she was feeling uneasy. As soon as I had an opportunity I tried to steer the conversation to a natural conclusion.

"These Emissaries you met, they sound very much like the people we are looking for," Ishtar suddenly said.

"Your description is very similar," I said. "And the fact that I met the Emissaries in your country, and now here you are in my country looking for the same type of community... it is all very intriguing."

"I believe you know where we need to go," he continued. "If you have been with the Emissaries, then perhaps you can find them again. Perhaps they left Croatia and came here."

I wanted to help them but I knew I couldn't. They were obviously on to something, but I also felt that they were not grounded enough to understand what they were really looking for. They seemed to be searching for a way out of the world, and judging from what they had experienced in their lives, that was no surprise. What I learned from the Emissaries had nothing to do with leaving the world, but with entering it fully. Ascension is not an escape, but the natural result of giving up all escapes. But how could I explain this to them? Their pain was so deep and their search was so vast that they had to find it out for themselves.

"I wish I could help you," I told them. "But I don't know anything about the Emissaries being here, or anywhere else."

Moments later Jennifer and I were at the car ready to leave.

"I feel sorry for them," Jennifer said as she opened the door.

"Why?"

"Because they're obviously very sincere. But it's also obvious that they aren't ready for whatever it is they're searching for. But then again, I probably would have thought the same thing about you if I had met you in Croatia."

Just then Maya ran to the car and handed me a piece of paper.

"This is Fr. John's phone number," she said. "Please call him when you can. I truly believe you are supposed to meet, no matter what you think of us."

From the moment we left Maya and Ishtar I felt the heaviness in my stomach increase till it was nearly unbearable. Something seemed to be trying to steer me away from them, and every time I thought of calling Fr. John the feeling intensified. I wanted to throw his phone number away and be done with the business. But what if he had the clue I was looking for? Circumstances seemed to be pulling me toward and away from him at the same time.

I decided to call Fr. John three days after our visit with Maya and Ishtar. Much to my amazement, as soon as he answered the phone I felt the heavy weight leave. I introduced myself and told him who had given me his number.

"Yes, Maya told me you might call," he said. "It sounds like you had quite an adventure in former Yugoslavia. I just bought your book *Emissary of Light,* but haven't had a chance to read it yet."

"According to Maya you have been to Bosnia as well," I said.

"Yes, several times. I was stuck in Sarajevo once during the war, then went back a year later to plant a peace pole at the exact spot where the Archduke Ferdinand was assassinated in 1914, sparking World War I. It appears the earth has a tendency to remember powerful events... on an energetic level of course, regardless of whether they're positive or negative. I believe that planting a peace pole and saying certain prayers can help neutralize a negative vortex and bring it back to normal. That has been one of the more bizarre areas of my work lately."

I then told him about the concert I was scheduled to perform in Belgrade. He explained that he had wanted to go to Serbia for a long time.

"There is a region of Serbia called Kosovo which is ready to explode in ethnic warfare at any time," he said. "In Kosovo there is a place called the 'Field of the Blackbirds' which has been an energetic point zero for all the negative events that have taken place there for the last six hundred years. During the later Crusades there was a battle on this small area of land and much of the Serbian army was slaughtered. It became their battle cry, 'Remember the Field of the Blackbirds,' and they've been saying it ever since. Almost every conflict in that region of the world has had some connection to that field. I believe it is because the land itself has not been healed. It is continually re-energized by the negative attention paid it by the Serbian people. I want to go there with a peace pole and conduct the same ceremony we did in Sarajevo. I believe we can heal the land, and in doing so, begin the healing of that whole region."

He definitely didn't talk like any priest I had ever heard before. Priests don't normally believe in things like 'healing the land', or 'negative energy vortexes'. If for no other reason than that, I knew I had to meet him. He agreed, and we decided that Jennifer and I would join him at his house the next evening.

"I read your book *Emissary of Light* today and must say that I am amazed," John said as soon as we arrived. He was a small man with wild unkempt hair, and wore a blue sweater with a medallion of the Blessed Mother hanging around his neck. His appearance made me think that we were in for a bit of a ride, but then I looked into his eyes and felt utter compassion, as if he radiated peace. We sat down with him at a kitchen table that stood in the center of his living room. It was covered with papers and the whole room was filled with books and photographs.

"What was it about the book amazed you?" I asked.

"Well, this may take some time to explain, but I feel it's important for you to get a full picture of who these people really are. Let me begin by asking you a couple of questions: Do you know where the Emissaries came from... or what spiritual lineage they claim?"

"Not at all," I told him. "They said that the Emissaries have existed in one way or another for thousands of years... that they are an ancient mystery school."

"That is correct, but do you know where or how they began?"

"No I don't... in fact I have often wondered that myself, but every time

I asked they wouldn't give me an answer. They said it wasn't important and that I should concentrate on what was."

"They may be right... but I personally believe that there is a reason to discuss their heritage further. Before we go into that I feel I should explain a few things. First of all, do you know the three basic commands Jesus gave to his apostles in the gospels?"

I was immediately taken aback by his question and wondered where he was leading me. It was as if our conversation had suddenly turned into a Bible history class.

"The first command was given to all the apostles at the Last Supper," John continued. "He told them to love one another unconditionally. Later he said to Peter, 'Feed my sheep.' Finally, during the crucifixion he said to John, 'This is your mother,' referring of course to Mary, and the gospel goes on to say that John took Mary into his home. These are the only times Jesus gave direct commands to his apostles."

"How does this apply to the Emissaries?" I asked.

"Let's look at the nature of these three commands," John said, as if I hadn't said a word. "The first command, his words to the apostles, were actually directed to the community of believers, what we would call the church. He was giving us, in very simple and public terms, the foundation of his whole teaching. The second command, the words he spoke to Peter were in truth spoken to the institution. The primary responsibility of the institutional church is to provide for the spiritual needs of the people.

"The most mysterious command is the one he gave to John," he continued. "Now you'll recall that John is referred to as 'the apostle whom Jesus loved.' This related to the deep mystical bond between Jesus and John, and that is the clue we are looking for. When he was dying on the cross Jesus said to John, 'Behold your mother,' and to Mary he said, 'Woman, behold your son.' We also know that John was the only apostle that wasn't martyred. It's clear that his role was special, that he had been put in charge of Jesus' most sacred relationship, the relationship he had with his mother."

I was becoming confused and had a hard time following him. There was still no direct link to the Emissaries, and that was the only reason I was listening. As intriguing as all this was, it wasn't getting me any closer to discovering the identity of the 'next teacher.'

"There's one more passage I want to remind you of," he continued without the slightest pause. "At the end of the fourth gospel, Peter looks at

John and says, 'Lord, and what shall this man do?' Jesus replies, 'If it should be my will that he wait until I come again, what is that to you?' Why would Peter ask this question? And more important, what did Jesus mean by this? There was something about the relationship between Peter and John that Peter never understood. Peter's role was to head the institution, and thus he became the first pope. But John's role was secret. He was given the care of Jesus' mother, and that is almost all we hear of him. The institution, of which Peter had the charge, had no idea what John's real role was.

"To continue that thought, most historians admit that the Gospel of John, the Letters of John, and the Book of Revelations, though they are all attributed to the same disciple, were actually written by two or three different people. It is believed that John founded a group called 'The Community of the Beloved Disciple,' and that members of this community, under the guidance of the saint, took his words and wrote them down. The last words Jesus spoke to John before his death became the foundation and focus of their lives: 'This is your mother.' They took her into their homes, or into their hearts, and then waited for the return of the Christ."

I began to see a pattern developing in his long winding path. The pieces were beginning to fall into place, and I needed just another moment of patience.

"What happened to this community?" I asked him.

"No one knows exactly. Some people believe they went underground, at least the more esoteric branches of the order. Later on many sects of the community were declared heretics and were massacred by the church. For example, the only nation to ever make this esoteric society its official religion was what we now know as Bosnia. They were called the Bogomils which means, 'the lovers of God.' The Cathars and Knights Templar were also members of the order, but they too were massacred. During the Dark Ages anyone who did not follow the established rite was either killed or forced to conform. It seemed that the esoteric order started by St. John was destroyed."

"But it wasn't, was it," I said as I finally saw where he was leading me. "You believe that the Emissaries of Light are part of that order, don't you?"

"It seems to make sense," John said as he stood up from his chair. "Maybe I should explain something. Though I am a priest, I have always known that I am also part of the 'Community of the Beloved Disciple.' I am, in the strictest sense of the word, a heretic in my own church. This is obviously not something I can talk about publicly, but it is true nonetheless. It has always been one of my goals to help reestablish the order. I also know that it has continued to this day, but only in total secrecy. It is a long-standing tradition that the communities pray for the evolution of humanity, as well as wait for the return of the Light of Christ. And this fits in perfectly with your Emissaries."

"And the fact that the Emissaries were in Bosnia makes sense as well," I said. "If what you said is true, that Bosnia was the only country where the society was the official religion, then it explains why the Emissaries were there."

"It's certainly true," he said. "Any of this can be looked up in any number of books. In fact, strictly speaking, they didn't even call themselves Bogomils. They simply called themselves Christians, and yet they had no hierarchy, no pope, and men and women were equal. Their faith and their lives were lived in utter simplicity. As a result they were a great threat to the institutional church, and from that perspective, had to be stopped. Bosnia, as you know, is sandwiched between Croatia and Serbia. The Croatian Catholics and the Serbian Orthodox persecuted the Bogomils terribly, and that persecution continues to this day."

"It sounds to me that the trouble started with Peter and John," Jennifer added. "That line from the gospel you mentioned before, that Peter should not be concerned with what Jesus had asked John to do… it's obvious that a division or some mild schism was created."

"That's correct," John said. "Right there on the last page of the gospel you have a clear distinction between the role of the outer church, headed by Peter, and the mission of the inner community, inspired by John. As the church grew and gained influence, it became increasingly difficult for the hierarchy to know what its more secret side was doing. Peter had the words of Jesus to confirm the role of John, but what happens a thousand years later when the church has become a corrupt political institution? For the next several hundred years the church launched various inquisitions to destroy these communities. That is what sent them underground, and so they have remained until today."

"The fact that I was brought to the Emissaries and asked to extend their teaching indicates that they're not to be kept secret anymore," I said.

"I agree," John said. "Just as Jesus says in the Gospel, the lineage of John would wait for the Second Coming of Christ. Your Emissaries spoke about a new teacher, the 'Messenger of Love.' I believe that this teacher, whoever it is, is the bearer of light we have been waiting for. The Emissaries have actually broken their silence, and like John the Baptist who prepared the way of Jesus, we have all been asked to prepare the way again."

I was suddenly overwhelmed by the importance of this discovery. When Teacher said to tell people that they are ready for the transformation that is at hand, he meant it quite literally. He said that people need to be activated to understand the coming revelation, otherwise it would pass them by. In the same way, John the Baptist went through Israel telling people to repent and prepare the way of the Lord. He too was activating people so they could hear the message of Jesus. Two thousand years later the same message is being heard again, not only through the Emissaries but all through the world.

"I have been waiting for an opportunity like this for a very long time," John said to me. "I believe that the Emissaries you met in the mountains of Bosnia are the most secret and elusive branch of the 'Community of the Beloved Disciple' founded by St. John. And I also believe that they know what we only suspect, that the time of the Second Coming is at hand. I also have a feeling I know who this 'new teacher' is, but I can't say anything about it yet. There is a woman I want you to meet, a shaman who lives here in Los Angeles named Shrinat Devi. I believe that she will know what we should do next. But we should wait until we're ready to leave for Serbia before we see her."

"I don't understand," I said. "Are you planning on coming with me?"

"I feel it's important that I go and plant a peace pole at the 'Field of the Blackbirds.' I think your concert is the perfect excuse, and once we are there we can do the real work. I also believe that we will be shown more about the 'next teacher' the Emissaries spoke of. That's really what you want, isn't it?"

I agreed and we decided to plan the trip together. The sudden change in direction startled me, but it felt right. There was something about Fr. John that completely intrigued me, and his knowledge about the lineage of St. John suddenly seemed invaluable. Jennifer and I said goodnight and I promised to call him the next day to arrange our visas and our flight.

(From a report submitted by Fr. John entitled: The Real Meaning of the Battle of Kosovo)

The battle of Kosovo took place on June 28, 1389 between a Christian Coalition led by Tsar Lazar of Serbia and the Turkish Muslim forces led by

King Murad. In addition to being a great leader, Tsar Lazar was also a very spiritual and holy man. In a story told to every Serbian school child for countless generations, an extraordinary event is recounted. The night before the battle the prophet Elijah, appearing in the form of a gray falcon, brought Tsar Lazar a message direct from the Blessed Mother, Mary: he could win either a great material or a great spiritual victory. It was his choice. If he chose the material victory and the Earthly kingdom, he and his troops would triumph on the battle field. If he chose the spiritual victory and the Heavenly Kingdom, they would all die. Being a man of profound Christian faith, Tsar did not hesitate and chose the spiritual victory. The next day the battle was lost and both Tsar Lazar and King Murad were killed.

The meaning of the promised spiritual victory was the letting go or death and defeat of ethnic and religious nationalism for the creation of something greater, a uniquely Balkan Muslim and Christian culture. Tsar Lazar's choice of the Heavenly Kingdom led eventually to the flowering of diverse religious and ethnic cultures, all living together in peace and mutual respect. This was most profound in Bosnia, and in Sarajevo in particular where the Roman Catholic cathedral, the old Mosque, the old Serbian Orthodox church and the Sephardic Jewish Temple were all within two hundred yards of one another. As such, Sarajevo became a model of hope for the future of the world and a bulwark against religious fundamentalism and fanaticism.

The failure by Serbian nationalists to understand the meaning of the spiritual victory and their reaction to the material loss have led to their attempts ever since to try to reverse or undo it — as if the battle had never been lost, as if the Muslims had never been in Kosovo, as if the hundreds of years of cultural flowering and unique legacy of Muslims and Christians living together had never occurred, as if Tsar Lazar had chosen the material victory instead of the spiritual victory. The monument to the Battle of Kosovo at the 'Field of the Blackbirds' became instead a symbol of Serbian ethnic and religious nationalism, the very values Tsar Lazar had repudiated in his choice of a spiritual victory. Serbia went against their greatest spiritual leader, his vow and choice, and the Blessed Mother's promise to him.

This led away from the fulfillment of their spiritual destiny for which Tsar Lazar's great sacrifice was intended, and toward the Serbs becoming the inadvertent agents of the forces of darkness with which they had unconsciously allied themselves. This turned their nation into an instrument or portal through which great evil would come into the world to their own ultimate harm and suffering, and that of others.

It is well known that World War I was triggered by the assassination of

Archduke Ferdinand in Sarajevo in June 1914 by a Serbian man named Gavrilo Princep. This in turn paved the way for World War II, the rise of the Adolph Hitler and the Nazi party, the Holocaust, and many other horrors. This has sometimes been referred to as the Great War from 1914–1945. The war in former Yugoslavia ended nearly a century of European warfare with ethnic violence that had not been seen since Hitler. What is not so well known are the links of all these events to Kosovo and the promise to Tsar Lazar.

Gavrilo Princep, a Serbian nationalist, specifically chose the day of June 28 to assassinate the ArchDuke. It was the anniversary of the Battle of Kosovo, but what he did not know was the true nature of the group working behind the scene that sponsored the assassination and from whom he took his direction. They were not the like-minded nationalists Princep thought they were, but a secret Serbian occult terrorist organization that called themselves "The Black Hand." In this light the events of 1914–1945 and their spiritual significance take on a whole new meaning.

The continuation of the forces unleashed by these events brings us back to Kosovo on June 28, 1989, the 600th anniversary of the battle. President Milosevic of Serbia, also the last president of Yugoslavia, gave an historic speech on the battlefield of Kosovo to rally the last vestiges of a greater material Serbia. This final tragic misinterpretation of the spiritual victory won at the Battle of Kosovo and God's promise to Tsar Lazar set into motion all the terrible events that have taken place in Bosnia, Croatia, Slovenia and now Kosovo over the last ten years. These have all been the dark fruits of the misunderstanding of the Battle of Kosovo.

Now at the turn of the millennium the Battle of Kosovo is being fought again. We pray that this time full conscious awareness will be applied to the significance of the first battle of Kosovo as well as its historical and spiritual consequence. Let us realize what is really at stake, so it will be the LAST time it needs to be fought. We pray that it will be fought through to the end, without a weakening of our spiritual resolve.

People speak of national interest, usually interpreted in political or economic terms. But there is a national soul and a national moral interest as well. It is in the natural soul interest of the soul of every nation, including and especially the soul of Serbia that is being defiled by Milosevic's actions and philosophy, that this evil be stopped.

week before John and I were scheduled to leave for Serbia I drove to Prescott, Arizona, to visit my dear friend Liz Story. She lived with her husband Joel atop a small mountain a few miles out of town, and it was a wonderful opportunity for me to relax and prepare for the journey that lay ahead. Liz is a world-renowned pianist, and each day as she practiced with the doors and windows swung open, I would walk through the forest with the music reverberating in my ears. It was like a dream, and I drank it in with great joy.

The heavy feeling returned a few days after my first visit with John. I thought that the fresh mountain air would take care of it, relieve whatever pressure was causing this discomfort. When it didn't I became concerned, wondering what was happening to me. It began the day Jennifer and I went to meet Maya and Ishtar, and it had come and gone constantly ever since. It seemed most pronounced every time I thought about the trip to Serbia. I was starting to feel that I wasn't supposed to go at all. But how could I know whether it was just my imagination or a true warning?

The morning I was scheduled to return to LA I looked out the window and saw that three feet of snow had fallen overnight. Liz and I were alone in the house and it soon was obvious that we were stranded. We tried for hours to get the car out of the long drive but it was no use. Two days passed and nothing changed. It was the day before I was to leave for Serbia, and it was beginning to look hopeless.

"I have been having similar difficulties," John said when I called him on the phone, "just not as drastic. I'm starting to think that there are forces that are trying to stop us from making this trip."

"What kind of forces are you suggesting?" I asked.

"I've already told you about the occult history of Serbia. These groups are still active there, and the last thing they want is for us to come and release whatever black magic they're practicing. Your snow storm may just be a coincidence, but I believe that they have the power to do such things if they want. These are forces we can't understand."

"It sounds crazy to me," I said. "But if what you're saying is true, then we've already lost. There doesn't seem to be any way to get down this mountain."

"That's not true. There are always more forces working for good than for evil. We have to pray and know that we will be taken care of. If we're supposed to go on this trip, then you will find a way to get here."

I hung up the phone and sat down on the couch. Liz was outside shoveling but I was already exhausted. My eyes closed and I said a short prayer. "If I'm meant to go on this trip, then get me off this mountain. I know you're more powerful than any negative forces that might be at play here. I want to go... I want to do this work. So if that's what you want as well, then help me do it."

Liz opened the door and brushed the snow off her coat. "I have an idea," she said. "There's a guy I know in town who owns a huge four wheel drive truck. I'll bet he can get up here, then he can take us both into town."

Liz called the man and by late afternoon we were back in Prescott. Once we got to town the roads were much better and I was able to get a lift to LA. I arrived at John's house around 1 a.m., twelve hours before our plane was scheduled to leave. For a moment the feeling in the pit of my stomach was gone and I felt I had won a victory. But would it last? I was starting to believe all the crazy stories John was telling me. Maybe there was more happening than I knew. I had never experienced anything like this on my other trips, regardless of the danger. This was different, somehow, and I was about to find out just how different it was.

Two hours before our flight was scheduled to leave Los Angeles, John announced that it was time for us to visit his friend Shrinat Devi. "She is a devoted Catholic as well as a shaman of the highest order," he explained. "She needs to pray with us before we leave. It's kind of a tradition of mine before I go on a journey like this."

We pulled up in front of a small house in a marginally poor neighborhood of Inglewood. As soon as we got out of the car I felt a strange sensation, as if we had just entered a bubble of light. John and I walked to the back entrance and knocked on the door. Seconds later a tall black woman with deep radiant eyes stood in front of us, and before we could say a word she took us both by the hand and led us to the front yard.

"The Mother has a message for both of you," she said. "You need to go with her blessing, for this is her work... she's the one who has called you on this journey."

As we turned the corner I saw a wooden shrine with the words "Queen of Peace" painted above a three-foot statue of Mary. Shrinat Devi literally pushed me to my knees in front of the statue and said: "You have to pray for guidance. Otherwise you may get hurt over there. This is a critical time for you and for the whole world. But if we all stick with her, we'll be fine."

Then she put one hand over my heart and the other on my back. "Fr.

John, pray the 'Hail Mary' with me three times," she said over her shoulder. I could hear the sound of their voices as they prayed, but I felt myself being pulled into an altered state, as if I were leaving that place and going somewhere completely new.

But it wasn't new at all. In fact, it was a very old place, a time from my past when I was young and naïve. I was suddenly back at Marytown, the friary near Chicago, praying before the statue of Mary that I loved so much. I could feel her presence, and tears of joy began running down my cheeks. It was as if I was in love, and my whole life was ahead of me. I wanted to merge with her light, her holiness and her grace. The experience enveloped me in a blanket of peace, and then filled me completely.

In the midst of this experience, I could feel Shrinat Devi lean over and place her mouth next to my ear. "That's right, honey, she's right there with you. She wants you to know that she hasn't forgotten you, even though you forgot her. This is the time she needs you most, and she has sent many angels to bring you back. She wants you to go to Medjugorje, the village in Bosnia where she appeared to the six little children. That's where you'll see her, and she'll give you the next direction. Do whatever it takes to get there, because that's where the miracle is going to begin."

Then she said something to me I will never forget: "Don't worry about anything, because Mary's going to take you through the Door. She's the one you've been waiting for."

The experience ended almost as soon as it began, and I nearly fell over backwards when she finally took her hands off my body. For several moments I couldn't move. I just sat there on the grass like a statue. Finally I looked up at her and asked: "Have you read my book *Emissary of Light?*"

"I don't read many books," she said. "I didn't even know you wrote a book."

"Then how did you know I was waiting for a teacher who would show me the Door of Eternity?"

"I only know what she tells me," she said. "That's all I need to know. You just do what the Mother wants you to do. You go to Medjugorje and see what she has in mind."

"You said something about a miracle," I said to her. "What miracle is going to begin there?"

"This is her time... her moment. This is the time of her awakening. Do you understand what I mean? She is calling many people to her aid right now, people who will help her initiate the next world. She needs you to find the one who bears the Light of Christ. That person is here right now waiting to be revealed. When you go to Medjugorje she will explain everything to you. It is a place of great spiritual importance and energy, and you must find a way to go there again."

I knew the village she spoke of very well. It was where my adventure with the Emissaries had ended, on a small hill where I had my last meeting with Teacher. He had reminded me about the Door, and he had spoken once more about the 'new teacher' who would come. It was there, in Medjugorje, that six children saw Mary, the Blessed Mother, beginning in 1981, and since then millions of people had flocked to the small village to be in her presence.

Mary had made many predictions during her apparitions in Medjugorje, about the coming war and what would happen if we did not turn back to God. Many of the predictions turned out to be true, but it was her message of peace that attracted me. She had said that an era of peace was coming, but only if we chose it. Otherwise we would experience a time of considerable challenge. I was personally moved by the energy I had felt there, very similar to what I experienced with the Emissaries. But I hadn't felt any overwhelming desire to return, at least not until that moment.

"It sounds like you're talking about the Second Coming," I said. "Do you mean that Jesus is about to return?"

"I said that the Light of Christ has already returned. And I didn't say anything about Jesus. She had two children, but the other has been asleep for a very long time. They are really the same, but manifest in two different ways. You are to find the second, which is really the first."

I looked over at John to see if he understood what she said. She couldn't possibly mean what it sounded like she was saying, that Mary had two children and one has been sleeping for two thousand years. It not only made no sense but would be considered a heresy, the type of thing people were killed for in earlier centuries.

"Don't try to interpret what I've said to you," she continued. "It's impossible for you to understand now. But you will, after you're with her. That's when it will all make sense. She will explain everything."

I looked over at John and motioned that it was time to go. What could I make of this visit, I wondered? Was I meant to take what she said literally, or was it some kind of mystical metaphor that would make sense later?

John seemed as confused as I was, but as he stood to say goodbye to Shrinat Devi she whispered something in his ear that only he could hear. John nodded, then turned to leave.

"What do you think of all that?" I asked when we got in the car.

"I'm not exactly sure," he said. "What she was saying about Mary having two children sounded very strange, but Shrinat Devi will often speak in code. She probably meant something very deep and mystical, but we'll have to wait to find out what it is."

"What did she whisper in your ear?"

"I suppose it really wasn't a secret," he said. "She said to make sure you get to Medjugorje, no matter what it takes. We'll have to talk about that later, because it may be tricky."

John and I left for Serbia an hour later and immediately began reviewing our plans. The problem was that we only had a single entry visa, and if we left Serbia, we would not be able to return. That would negate the reason we were making this journey — to plant the peace pole in Kosovo. But I felt the truth in what Shrinat Devi had said to me. I knew she was right... I could feel it in my bones. One way or another I had to get into Bosnia, then find my way back to Medjugorje. I knew that Mary would take care of the details, that is, of course, if she really did want me.

Sometime during the flight to Serbia the pain in my stomach returned. The closer we got to our destination the stronger it felt, and I was afraid that I was going to be sick. I told John about my concern and he tried to put me at ease.

"I think our suspicions about the energy of Serbia were correct," he said. "As soon as we crossed into Serbian air-space I felt the heaviness myself, as if there's a huge black glove hovering over the entire country blocking the light. I am starting to think that the work of the occult society I mentioned before is stronger than I anticipated. They don't want us here at all, as if our presence is a great threat to their work."

"What are we going to do about it?" I asked him.

"We're going to do what we came to do. You'll perform your concert and pray the peace prayers. Then we'll go to Kosovo and plant the peace pole. It is important that we leave as soon as possible when we have finished our work. These things have a tendency to swing back around, like an energetic backlash. We don't want to put ourselves at more risk than we need to."

"What can we do to protect ourselves?"

"We should stay together, no matter what happens," he said. "The forces that don't want us in Serbia will try to separate us because it will decrease our effectiveness. We can't let that happen."

"There's only one thing I'm concerned about," I said. "Shrinat Devi told me that I had to go back to Medjugorje because Mary has a message for me. But if we leave Serbia we won't be able to return. It seems to me that it will be hard for us to do both, but that both are critically important."

"All I can say is that we must stay together," he said. "I believe that above all else we must go to the Field of the Blackbirds. If we are going to release the negative energy that is present in Serbia, it must happen there."

W e arrived in Belgrade and found ourselves in the midst of an amazing revolution. Nanad, the man who was meant to plan the peace concert, met us at the airport. John and I carried the six-foot long peace pole packed tightly in a box, barely making it through customs. There were pictures of the pole taped everywhere on the outside of the box, a strategy to put their minds at ease since we didn't want them thinking we were smuggling a cannon into their country.

"I am sorry to greet you with bad news," Nanad said as we passed through the customs door. "Your peace concert has been canceled. Things are very difficult here right now, and we have no choice. It is a decision of the government."

Nanad was a large, well-built man with striking white hair. His eyes were warm and he had a friendly face, but I couldn't hide my disappointment.

"What do you mean it's a decision of the government?" I asked. "I thought everything was arranged."

"It was," he said, taking the peace pole from the two of us as if it were no heavier than a baseball bat. "The daily marches have the government in a panic and they cannot afford to let you sing here. It will only cause them more trouble."

"I thought that Milosevic gave in to their demands," John said. "Why do they continue to march if they've achieved their goal?"

"Many Serbs will not be happy until they have forced him out of office. As I said, these are very trying times, especially after the war in Bosnia. And now things are not going well in Kosovo. It seems there is no end to the trouble."

The Belgrade night was cold and dark, and the air was filled with the peculiar scent of a city without hope. John said he had felt this ominous cloud the moment we entered Serbian air space, while we were still in the jet. It felt very much like Sarajevo, I thought, but without the bombs and burned out buildings. And yet the energy was the same, the same despondency I have felt in other countries torn apart by hatred and greed.

Nenad had booked us a room at a hotel somewhere on the outskirts of Belgrade. We drove through the dark streets past long lines of men standing with empty faces. I tried to figure out what they were doing standing together looking so cold. And yet I could feel them, their confusion and their hard impenetrable hearts. It made the feeling in my stomach hurt and grow, and I wasn't sure how much longer I could take it.

The hotel looked fine enough from the outside, but when we opened the door to our room my heart sank. The dark cubicle had one small window and four beds. That was all. There was no bathroom, only a sink that could not be turned off, and a steam heater that was dead cold. The only toilet was down the long hall and on another floor. It had not been cleaned for days and was broken. That fact, however, did not seem to stop people from continuing its use.

Thankfully, John and I had the room to ourselves, though the hotel clerk made it clear that we were likely to get a roommate at any time. It's the way it is, he said to us, hotel policy, and there was nothing he could do about it. As I fell onto the hard mattress I began to feel as if something was seriously wrong with me. And yet it seemed it wasn't my body that was in trouble, but my soul. It felt as if something had wrapped itself around me, making it hard to breathe or even move. My head began to ache and a sense of dread grew deep within me. All I could think about was leaving, as soon as possible. And yet we had only just arrived. There was nowhere for us to go.

"There is an entity trying to possess you," John said to me. "Most priests don't believe in things like possession any more, but I have actually seen it happen. This kind of spiritual intervention work we're engaged in attracts this energy, like a demonic force that will do anything to see us fail. It seems to have attached itself to you in particular, though I have been feeling them as well. They can't get to me quite as easily because I have been doing this work longer. I know how to protect myself."

"You've got to do something," I said, reaching out for his hand. I was already exhausted and could feel my sanity slowly slipping away from me. The fear I felt was overwhelming. It took every ounce of energy I had to hold on and stay conscious. The room seemed to be closing in on me, and the sound of the running faucet was nearly driving me out of my mind.

"Whatever you do," he said, "don't let yourself lose consciousness. Listen to my voice and stay with me. I am going to pray over you and try to sever the connection. Tell me how long you have felt the attack."

"Since I first met Maya and Ishtar," I said. "It has come and gone since then."

"Where in your body is the feeling strongest?" he asked.

"In the area around my stomach. I can hardly breathe."

"Take slow, steady breaths," he said as he stood over my bed. "The entity is trying to steal your power. It believes that it can make you leave Serbia and let it continue oppressing the people here. There are legions of demons blocking the light. I want you to keep your eyes open and keep breathing. I am going to do what I can."

His voice suddenly seemed very far away from me. I saw him put a priest's stole around his neck and take out a small black prayer book. He made the sign of the cross over me and began to pray. The words echoed in my head and I strained to hear him. What is he saying, I wondered? Now and then I felt myself falling asleep, then I felt John's hand shake me gently, bringing me back.

"Stay with me," he said. "It's beginning to work."

His hand was now on my forehead, then I felt him trace the sign of the cross with his thumb over my skin. My stomach suddenly went numb, as if a weight was being pressed against it. John stepped back and began waving his arms in the air, speaking in a language I didn't understand. His voice grew louder until he was nearly screaming. My head was pounding and I remember thinking I would die.

I looked up and saw a most terrifying vision. Something like a dark cloud seemed to leave my body, hovering there for a moment as if it was trying to get back inside me. John seemed to notice it as well, and he stared at it with an intensity I had never seen in him before. The prayers continued and he now made the sign of the cross again and again in front of the dark mass. I watched in disbelief, unable to move or even breathe. Part of me couldn't believe my own eyes, as if I had really fallen asleep and was having a terrible dream. But it wasn't a dream — it was real, and there was nothing I could do about it.

Then suddenly, without warning, it was over. The dark form had vanished and John closed the book. He made the sign of the cross one final time, then stepped toward me.

"Now you can sleep," he whispered in my ear. "Everything is going to be fine. We can discuss it in the morning."

Sleep. I needed sleep. But how could I? My senses must be playing tricks on me, I decided. Yes... what else could it be? The alternative was too horrifying to be true.

7 awoke to the sound of car horns on the busy street below. The light streamed in through the window and for the first time I could really see the condition of our room. It was worse than I remembered. The wallpaper was peeling from the walls and the ceiling had three holes in it. Luckily we were still alone — no other guest had arrived the night before. And yet the activities, for lack of a better description, from the night before had drained me, and I resisted the idea of getting up at all. Just then the door opened and John walked in.

"Greetings Jimmy," he said. "I'm glad to see you're awake. I didn't want to disturb you so I went out to explore for awhile. How do you feel?"

"I feel like I have a hangover," I said to him. "And I hardly remember what happened. It's like a dream."

"That doesn't surprise me. In a way it was. You were under psychic attack — real heavy stuff. I don't know what would have happened if I hadn't intervened, but it was definitely touch and go."

"So it's true," I said, surprised. "Something was trying to break me down, and it almost worked. But why?"

"You know why. We're not supposed to be here, at least not from the perspective of those who are trying to work evil. If we plant this peace pole in Kosovo and do the ceremony I have planned, then things will have to shift here. But things don't want to shift, that's the problem. The oppressive energy you felt last night is commonplace — people don't even notice it. Imagine getting so used to the rain that you forget what the sun looks like. That's what it's like, but now it has to change."

"I feel as if something has lifted off me," I said, "as if it's gone, whatever it was."

"It is gone. I can tell by looking at you that we've cleared the energy around you. The question is, are you willing to do what it takes to keep it clear?"

"What do you mean?"

"If we're going to complete this mission, then we have to stay focussed. I believe the entity, or whatever it was, that had attached itself to you did so because you weren't clear. This work we're doing is very tricky, and it's important to be single-minded. Otherwise you can be drawn in lots of different directions... not all of them good."

"What do you suggest we do?" I asked.

"First of all, let's get out of this hotel. I don't care how much it costs but we need to take care of ourselves. The energy of this place is very low and oppressive, and that makes our job so much harder. We'll go downtown and find whatever we can."

"Then what?"

"Then we'll wait," he said. "We'll wait for a sign. Something is going to happen that will show us the next direction. Several doors have closed in our faces, and that means that others are ready to reveal themselves. We need to be attentive so we can recognize them when they do."

We packed our things and checked out. As soon as I was on the street I felt different, as if we had turned a corner, and oh, how welcome that feeling was. When we got downtown we set out to find a reasonable replacement, but at that point anything would have been better than where we had been the night before. The Hotel Carnival was the first we found and we were able to negotiate a reasonable rate.

We checked into the downtown hotel and collapsed on our beds. I felt as if we had hit a brick wall, as if we had misinterpreted the signs. We didn't say a word to each other for several minutes, just lay there looking up at the ceiling.

"Maybe we're supposed to go to Medjugorje like Shrinat Devi said," I ventured.

"But if we go to Bosnia now, we may not be able to get back into Serbia," John said. "And that means we will miss the chance to plant the peace pole in Kosovo... and that's the real reason we're here."

I sensed that John was afraid of something that he could not bring himself to say, probably of me leaving him and going on to Medjugorje alone. But there was something about what Shrinat Devi had said to me, something in the tone of her voice that convinced me she was right. I did need to go back to Bosnia, and though I didn't want to leave John, it was starting to seem that we were here on different missions after all.

Not more than ten minutes after we checked into our hotel we heard the sound of music coming from the street. It rose through the air and entered our room like a friend, a familiar voice that instantly soothed my ailing nerves. The music, which we immediately recognized as the Beatles' "Twist and Shout," grew louder till we went out onto the balcony to have a look. It couldn't be a car stereo, which is what I first thought. It was too loud for that.

The first thing we saw was a Jeep with a metal scaffolding built around its chassis, and balanced on the metal frame were four huge speakers facing in different directions. Behind the Jeep, an amazing number of people marched and danced their way toward us. There were easily ten thousand women and men carrying banners and singing. They were like an enormous wave, and I felt my adrenaline catapult me out of the room and down the stairs. John was right behind me, and within seconds we were in the crowd, completely engulfed by the mass.

It seemed more like a party than a demonstration. The feeling of thousands of people, many of whom did not even speak English, dancing down the street singing, "Now shake it up baby... twist and shout," was amazing, even a little surreal. We could have been anywhere, with any group of young people, but the fact that we were in Belgrade demonstrating against an oppressive dictator was almost too much for me. I felt the excitement building, and I had to know what was happening.

"We realized months ago that Milosevic was not going to use force to stop us," a student told me. "NATO is right next door in Bosnia and would never let him get away with it. So we made it a huge party. Everyday thousands of people take over the street... we dance and we sing our songs. Then we go home. And we will continue this party until he gives in to us."

We talked with many students that day and heard the same story. They were taking to the streets with joy, not anger — and the government didn't know what to do. At one point we came to a large brick building that seemed to be covered in a strange sticky substance. The huge crowd stopped and began blowing whistles that were so shrill I had to cover my ears. I just stood there looking at the building, wondering what the glistening substance was.

"This building is the Ministry of Media," I was told. "It is controlled by the government and produces all the television programming available in Serbia. Three days ago everyone brought an egg and we threw them at the building. You should have seen it... thousands of eggs flying at one time and splattering in unison."

I was amazed at the humor that dominated this gathering. I remembered participating in several demonstrations years before when I was a member of the Catholic Worker community. Those events, in contrast, were more like funerals than rallies. The seriousness and conviction they conveyed always seemed to blanket the real goal. In Belgrade, which was more serious than anywhere I had ever been, a playful attitude permeated everything, and it threw the authorities an unexpected curve.

After walking with the group for another mile or so we turned a corner and everything suddenly changed. A large ornate government building loomed a block ahead of us, and in front of the building row after row of soldiers in riot gear stood guard. Each of them held a plexiglas shield half the size of their bodies in one hand, and a large wooden club in the other. I was beginning to wonder if our luck had changed when suddenly the huge crowd stopped in its tracks and stood very still.

A tall man with long dark hair and beard stood on the jeep and began speaking to the crowd through a microphone. "He is telling us how important it is to hold the peace," a student said to me. "We are conducting a non-violent revolution and must prove that we deserve what we are demonstrating for."

I could feel the cold sweat forming on my brow, and a knot of fear settled in my stomach. The throng was filled with young and old alike, all crowded together like a herd of sheep ready to jump off a cliff. Their commitment to changing their condition was evident, but so was their naïveté. They were either going to be heroes or get slaughtered, and I was right in the middle of everything.

When the man finished his speech, the crowd moved into an instant formation. Row after row formed, each one a half block long, and they marched straight toward the soldiers. I was suddenly afraid that I was going to witness a massacre, but nothing could have been further from the truth. They walked directly up to the soldiers and did something that defied belief — each one of them reached out their hands and touched the soldiers' shields, then looked them straight in the eyes and smiled. That was all. When they were finished, the next row did the same, on and on for nearly a half-hour, till everyone in the crowd, including myself, had had a turn.

I had not been sure whether to join them or not. After all, this was not my war and I wondered if it would be seen as an insult. But my feet seemed to have a mind of their own and before I knew it I was standing in front of a young brown haired soldier who tried hard not to look into my eyes. But he finally did, and something happened to both of us. Just for an instant we looked at one another, and I could feel how afraid he was. I realized that we were not so far apart.

Fr. John and I marveled about the events of that day as we lay in our room later that night. We were very much the same, the priest and I. Would I have been like him if I had continued on the path I had chosen when I was eighteen? Would I have been able to resist conforming to the mold that was set before me, the pious model of what was expected of a servant of the Church? Or would I have been more like my friend who was listening to a higher call, sent to witness the horrors of injustice and brutality, putting his own life at risk? I wondered if his own colleagues understood him. Did they dismiss him as a rebel and a lunatic, or did they see who he really was, the committed visionary who couldn't be locked inside any institution?

The demonstrators passed our hotel again the next day, but this time Fr. John wanted to remain behind. I decided not to talk to many of the students, just walk beside them and observe their heroism. I had learned so much the day before and felt inclined to keep a bit of distance.

After a few blocks I noticed a young blonde woman walking beside me. She seemed to be alone and I felt an overwhelming desire to speak with her. At first I was taken aback by this feeling since just moments earlier I had decided to be alone, and because I had no intention of getting 'involved' with anyone. But the feeling was so strong, and I knew I had to do something. I simply couldn't resist her. She was radiant, the most beautiful woman I had ever seen... of that I was sure. I finally tried to get her attention, but she didn't seem to notice me at all.

"Do you speak English?" I finally asked, leaning into her line of vision.

"Yes, I do," she said as she turned toward me and smiled.

"Are you a student here?" I waited for a long pause, yet there was no answer, so I tried again. "My name is Jimmy. I'm from... "

"Yes, I know where you are from. But why are you here, that's what I was wondering?"

I was stunned by her sudden inquiry, and yet she seemed to inspire a strange energy that completely overwhelmed me. It wasn't a conscious feeling as much as an instant recognition. I didn't know what to say, as if I had suddenly forgotten why I was there.

"I'm here to plant a peace pole in Kosovo," I said finally, "and to sing in a concert which seems to have been canceled."

"Why do you say it has been canceled?" she asked.

"Everything is changing here, and I don't know what to think. All I know is that I came here to perform, but the people who were supposed to have arranged the concert are nowhere to be found."

"Maybe you came here for a reason you have yet to discover," she said. "Maybe it will surprise you."

"What is your name?" I asked her.

"My name is Maria," she said, then smiled as if she was about to say more, but she never did.

"You seem different from the other students," I told her, anxious to continue the conversation. "You haven't said much, but I feel a depth that I didn't sense in my other conversations with people."

"What do you mean by depth?"

"I'm not sure really... I guess I can't explain it. Call it intuition, as if I can tell something about you without you saying it."

In all truth, I think I was hitting on her... though I didn't really notice it myself. Part of me felt an unfathomable distance from this angel who had suddenly appeared before me, and the rest of me seemed wholly focused on closing that gap. I was falling deeply in love with her, and that fact defied logic. There I was walking down this busy Serbian street with thousands of other people, and yet my mind was completely focused on one thing: Maria. Who was she, I wondered? Where had she come from and how was she inspiring this sudden devotion?

"There is a great deal more to discover," she said. "Do not trust what appears before your eyes because the truth lies past the gaze. Look behind the appearance and you will perceive something which is much closer to the truth."

"What do you mean?" I asked, stunned. I had not expected words like these, even though the energy was so strong.

"There is a truth which you cannot see," she continued, "here or anywhere else. You look around yourself and you see students who seem to be fighting for their rights. But that is a very narrow perspective, a very small picture compared to what is really happening. They are really searching for themselves, but they don't realize it. They have not learned to look within to discover reality, so they look to the world. Ultimately the world will fail them and they will be forced to look deeper. Then they will see with different eyes and understand what lies past their senses."

She spoke as if she were completely isolated from the other students in the crowd, as if she had nothing to do with them. Yet on the surface there was no discernible difference between Maria and the others, except for the insight that seemed so natural, so clear that there was no doubting its authenticity.

"You seem to have a very deep understanding," I said to her, completely perplexed. "How have you come to such a profound perspective?"

"I'm sorry, but I must leave now," she said as she reached out her hand to say good-bye. "It has been nice talking to you."

"Wait a minute," I said, tightening my grip on her hand. The thought of her leaving so suddenly was impossible to bear. "Where do you have to go? Can't you stay a little longer?"

"I cannot. But you will see me again. It will happen... I promise you."

She wrested her hand from mine and seconds later disappeared in the crowd. I watched her as she slipped in between several students, and then was gone. For a moment I wondered what had happened. Who was Maria and why did she say the things she did, only to leave so suddenly? And how could I possibly find her again in this crowd? There were thousands of people crammed onto a single street. It would take a miracle to find her again.

I spent the rest of that day lost in a strange melancholy. The protest no longer interested me, and I was unmoved by the enormity of the events that took place in front of my eyes. All I could think of was Maria, and the realization that she had to be wrong; there was no way I would see her again. It was nearly impossible, and besides, I was ashamed of the way I had launched myself at her. It was the only way I could explain her sudden disappearance. If I had only gone slower, I thought, maybe she would still be with me. But as it stood I was alone, and I couldn't see any reason to stay.

That night at dinner John and I made a decision. He finally agreed that I should follow Shrinat Devi's recommendation and go to Medjugorje. We were not able to get permission to plant the large peace pole in Kosovo, so we decided that John would go there alone and plant a six-inch pole in its place. (We had brought it along as a backup plan.) I would take the six-foot pole to Medjugorje and hopefully get permission to plant it there. I decided not to even try and find Maria. It was easier to forget all about her and get back to the real reason I was there. Our time was growing short and a decision had been made. As I got on the bus heading out of Serbia the next morning, I tried to clear my mind of every thought of Maria and concentrate on what lay ahead. It took most of the journey, and I nearly succeeded.

I could feel something building inside me, as if the decision to go to Medjugorje had triggered the next level of my adventure. I knew that Shrinat Devi was right. I could feel it, but I didn't have any way of knowing what it meant. It had something to do with Mary, the Blessed Mother; but then again, nearly everyone came to this little village with similar aspirations. Shrinat Devi said that Mother Mary was the one I was waiting for, and that she would take me through the Door of Eternity. Everything Teacher had said about the "Messenger of Love" flooded my mind, and I hoped I was about to find out what he meant.

I arrived at the village and immediately set about devising my strategy. The streets were filled with pilgrims and the small tourist shops were overflowing. I was never sure how to take this sort of spiritual extravaganza. The fervent attitude of the people was certainly inspiring, but something was definitely lost to the merchandising zeal. Every shop seemed to carry the same merchandise, a wide assortment of plastic rosaries and cheap ceramic statues. The most horrendous item, to my taste, was the three-dimensional picture of Jesus hanging on the cross. The face, oddly enough, would change depending upon the angle of approach. Stand to the left and his eyes were closed as if he had expired. Stand to the right and the eyes spring open with a startling and disconcerting suddenness. It must have been a good seller since every store had a full stock.

I went to the rectory as soon as I arrived in Medjugorje. As I sat in the waiting room I looked around at the pictures of Mary that lined the wall. Was this the room where she had appeared to the children after the government forbade access to the Hill of the Apparition? It felt strange to be holding my six-foot pole bearing the words, "May Peace Prevail on Earth" in English, Croatian, Serbian, and Muslim script. I wondered if those who saw it would understand our intent — to foster unity and understanding. Would the powers that be let us place it in a prominent location? As it turned out, I did not have enough time to go through the proper channels. I only had two days, and it just wasn't enough time to get official permission.

But we had formulated a backup plan. John and I had decided that it wasn't important that the pole be in a public place, as long as it was there. I would find a place away from the eyes of the thousands of pilgrims, a special spot that God would lead me to. And when I found that spot I would plant the pole in the earth, knowing that it would serve as an invisible beacon, demonstrating the importance of compassion and understanding. The next morning I would climb the Hill of the Apparition with the pole and wait to be led to the predestined spot.

I followed the path that millions of pilgrims had worn into the ground, up the hill to the spot where the miracle of Medjugorje began. I walked in silence until I felt compelled to leave the path and venture through the brush. When I came to the seventh station I suddenly found myself walking to the left, as if there was an unseen force leading me. The rocks were large and loose, and constant care had to be taken not to trip and fall. It felt like the pole was a crucifix, and I was carrying it to my own destiny. Huge thorn bushes formed a nearly impenetrable barrier, but I wound my way from the path and waited for a sign. After a hundred yards I still felt nothing. Something has to happen, I thought to myself. There needs to be an omen of some kind. But the silence of the hill felt heavy and ominous, and I began to wonder if I was in the right place at all.

Then something stole my attention. There was a strange sound near my leg, and when I looked down I saw a small collie which had silently found its way to my side. I set the pole on the ground and knelt down beside the dog.

"I didn't even hear you," I said. "Maybe you're my omen."

The dog looked like a miniature Lassie, and I sat on the ground to pet her. What kind of a sign is this, I wondered to myself? What does Lassie symbolize? Just then I heard bells ringing somewhere in the distance, as if angels were beginning to descend on the hill. Then I heard a voice that seemed to be coming from our left, just over the hill.

"Lassie! Lassie!" I couldn't believe my ears. I looked around and saw a herd of goats come up over the hill with a large round woman just behind holding a long stick. She was calling her dog, which oddly enough was named Lassie. She saw me petting the dog and stopped, but continued to call the dog's name. Lassie, on the other hand, seemed to be enjoying the attention I was giving her, and even when I ceased my petting, she would not leave my side.

"Maybe we're supposed to go to the woman," I said to the dog. "Maybe that's part of the omen."

I walked over to the woman and Lassie followed me. The woman seemed shy, and I suspected she didn't want to talk to tourists. Then I noticed that we were standing on top of a huge flat boulder that revealed a stunning view of Medjugorje far below. I could see St. James' Church and the whole region. Then I looked down at my feet. Just to my right was a hole in the rock the exact size of the peace pole. It slid in perfectly, and I stood there stunned, looking out over the land.

After the woman left with her goats, I sat down on the rock to pray. I expressed my gratitude for having been led to this place and asked Our Lady to bless the pole. I could feel the energy that rose from the earth, as if the ground itself was thankful for the gift. After a few moments I secured it in its hole, said a prayer, then left. As I walked down the hill I wondered if John had been successful in getting into Kosovo and carrying out his role in this strange drama. We were together even though we were apart, bound by the same mission. I had planted the peace pole in Medjugorje, and that was what I came to do. I would leave the next day for Rome, and John and I would meet again.

I thought about the pole that entire day. It seemed to be calling me back to the hill, as if it wanted company, someone to sit by its side and pray. Late in the afternoon I decided to visit it one last time, to look out over the landscape and breathe in that sacred air. As I prepared to return to the hill I wondered why I felt so connected to this strange and violent land. It was my third trip to former Yugoslavia, and each visit was so unique, beginning with the Emissaries. This journey was no exception, and I wondered if it was because the whole area had once vibrated with the teachings of St. John's mystical community. It was a thousand years earlier that the Bogomils, the Lovers of God, had preached their unique form of Christianity, a church that taught equality and forbearance above everything. They were killed for their faith, and the bloodbath had continued ever since. Maybe this beacon atop this tiny hill would help remind people of their ancient heritage. As I began walking toward the hill I prayed this might be possible.

I climbed the hill and ventured through the thorn bushes and loose rocks. Minutes later I was at the pole and sat down to meditate. It was late afternoon and I could feel the sun falling behind me. In a few moments it would disappear behind the hill, and then the light would begin to fade. I wondered if I would be able to find my way down the hill in the dark. It looked as if I still had an hour of daylight. After that it would be a dangerous descent.

Then I heard something behind me, like the sound of someone stepping on loose rocks. At first it was hard to tell what it was, but I soon realized that someone was actually coming down the hill and walking in my direction. I turned around but the sun was in my eyes and I could only make out the figure of a woman. I decided to wait for her to get near, then look again. Why would anyone risk themselves on this dangerous terrain, especially at this time of day? I thought I was the only one without enough sense to go home before dark.

I could hear the sound of footsteps very close behind where I sat. If I waited much longer she would be at my side, and I wanted to look before then. When I turned it took a few seconds for my eyes to adjust, then I saw her. I gasped when I realized who it was, as if all the air had suddenly gone out of me. My eyes widened and I couldn't move.

"Hello. Do you remember me?" she smiled.

It was Maria, from the march in Belgrade. But that was impossible. She was a student in Serbia, and it would be nearly impossible for a Serb to get into Bosnia so close to the end of the war. And besides, even if she could, the chances of seeing her on a hill in a tiny village hundreds of miles from Belgrade were nearly impossible. And yet, as impossible as it seemed, there she was, standing no more than ten feet from my side. She wore a brown suede jacket, jeans and leather boots. Her long hair was straight and blonde, falling loose behind her long thin neck. I suddenly felt the same overwhelming sensation that accompanied our meeting in Serbia, and it was then that I realized what was really happening.

"Maria," I gasped. "But it can't be. You're... "

There was a long moment of silence while we looked at each other. Her smile never faded, and neither did my amazement. Then the wind blew between us and sent a sudden chill up my spine. It made me shake for a second, just enough to awaken me from the trance of her gaze.

"Why are you surprised to see me?" she said as she sat down on a rock just to my right. "I promised that we would meet again... why not here in Medjugorje? This seems like an appropriate place."

"I can't believe it," I said as my head began to spin. "You're Maria... Mary... you're... " My words weren't adequate. No words were adequate. The possibility seemed so incredibly unbelievable.

She smiled gently. "Once again, why are you so surprised? You knew I would come, you knew in so many ways. You felt me coming, just as I have always felt you. You made a promise to me a very long time ago, when you were just a child. You have forgotten that promise, but I haven't."

"What was it I promised?" I asked after long seconds of silence.

"You asked to become an instrument of peace. Do you remember? You were only twelve years old sitting outside the church waiting for your mother to pick you up. You said that you wanted to give yourself to me and to be used to bring people to God. I have been with you every moment of your life, and have waited to come to you. I could never forget a promise like that."

"But why have you come in this physical way?" I asked, suddenly overwhelmed by the realization of who was sitting next to me. "You're as solid as I am. You're completely ordinary, but in another way, wholly Divine." As I said these words I realized how inappropriate I had been in Belgrade. If I had only known, I thought to myself. She seemed to read my thoughts and smiled again.

"God always works in ways we can understand. To six Croatian children who know only their catechism, I appear as the Queen of Peace holding a rosary. To you... well, you can see that it's different. But the message is always the same. I have come to call people back to God, to ask them to convert their lives. But people don't understand what that means. Often they believe it means sacrifice and penance, but in reality it means to accept love over fear. To sacrifice and deny yourself engenders and promotes fear, it doesn't release it. God asks only that you release the blocks that have kept you away from love... that have kept you from realizing that you are one with the Divine. You have never been separate, not even for an instant, except in your imagination. It is time to release those ideas and come home. Then you will realize that love is your inheritance... that you are a Child of God."

"This sounds very much like the message I received from the Emissaries in the mountains of Bosnia," I said.

"This same message is being expressed in many ways, by many people. And this is the essence of what you have heard: When you discover the Divine within another, in whoever is right in front of you, then you discover it within yourself. You often look for God in the extraordinary, in fantastic phenomena. But the miracle is not outside you, it is within. *You, all of you*, are the miracle, and when you look to the essence of another, you perceive it in yourself. That is the message of God, and it has always been my message. You will find God in the ordinary, in the smile of a child, by looking into the eyes of someone you have never met and not being afraid, when you hold the door open for an extra few seconds while you wait for someone to enter. That's how love is revealed in your life, that's how you will find the Door you're searching for."

"The Emissaries said that I would meet another teacher," I said to her. "Are you the one they spoke about?"

"Listen very close because what I am about to tell you is very important. I have not come for you alone, but for all the world. This is the dawn of the world of compassion and peace. I am the Queen of Peace because I fully embody these qualities, and I can assist your entry into this experience. You could say that I am the Feminine Principle. These qualities are traditionally feminine qualities, and it is into this energy that humanity must now enter. I can help in special ways, but only if you set aside the need to find peace through conflict. Compassion, understanding and tolerance are the paths that lead to me. This is the Door that humanity stands in front of."

"But what about those who are not Catholic... or Christian?" I asked. "Do people need to accept you in this particular role, or any particular religion?"

"I am not reserved for one particular group or religion," she said. "I am for the whole world, though many will find their own way of relating to me. The form is not important, but the energy is. It is the energy I bring that is important, and anyone can access it. If humanity is able to make this shift into the feminine energy, then peace will begin to sweep over the whole planet. But if you cling to power and domination, then you will miss this incredible opportunity, and you will continue to live in conflict."

I do not know how long we sat there, but I began to feel the cool wind on my neck and noticed that the sun had dipped behind the hill. It was the first time since she sat down next to me that I was aware of my body. Maria seemed to notice my discomfort and stood up as if she were going to leave.

"I still have a great deal more to tell you," she said. "But it will have to wait. I want you to begin cultivating these qualities in your own life. Live in compassion, breathe peace, teach only love, and you will start to sense the coming transformation. The next step will be revealed later, when you are ready. And because I know you will doubt what has happened here today, I am going to give you a sign that will put you at peace. In a very short time the whole world will see me flash through the sky with a tail of light. When you see this sign, know that the time is at hand when all the things I spoke of will come to pass. For now, never forget your promise to me, and know that I will never forget you."

She turned and began to walk up the hill in the same direction from which she had come. I tried to speak, but no words came. I still couldn't believe it was happening, that Maria, whoever she was, had spoken to me as if we had been friends forever. In that instant I knew that my life would never be the same. I would never be able to go back to the way things were, or my old way of thinking. Then, just as it was becoming difficult to see her in the dark, she turned around and faced me again.

"The reason I am with you like this is because my whole teaching is contained in this form. Find God in the ordinary. Seek the Divine in each other, and within yourself. That's how the transformation begins. That's how you'll remember who you are — the Sacred Self that God perceives. Come here again tomorrow and we'll talk more. There's still so much you need to learn, especially about the one who is coming... the bearer of light."

"I thought you were the one I was waiting for," I said to her. "Aren't you the 'next teacher' the Emissaries spoke of?"

"The next teacher is already with you, and you will know what to do when that time comes. I am here to prepare you. I am here to remind you of your promise, and to hold your hand. Don't worry, it will all make sense very soon."

Then she turned around and disappeared over the top of the hill. I thought about how appropriate that was — she didn't float toward the heavens, or vanish before my eyes. She simply walked away, just as ordinary as anyone else. And yet it really was her, the embodiment of every grace we have ever dreamed, the 'Messenger of Love' the Emissaries spoke of. And yet she said she wasn't the teacher I was told about, and this confused me. The 'Messenger of Love' and the 'next teacher' were two different people? Just when I thought I was beginning to understand, I found myself back at the beginning.

I began walking down the hill toward the rooming house where I was staying. It felt as if I was floating on air, flying down the hill over the rocks and thorns. When I got to the bottom I noticed a small chapel to my left, and in the courtyard of that chapel was a large statue of the Blessed Mother, the same statue Shrinat Devi had in her front yard, the same statue carved from the six children's description. I stopped for a moment to say a prayer of gratitude, and when I looked at the stone face, I nearly fainted. It was her, Maria, just as real as she had been only moments before. It was as if she herself had posed as a model while the statue was being carved. But why was I surprised?

I spent the whole evening at St. James, the parish church in Medjugorje, praying and trying to understand what had just happened to me. But how could I? There was no way to logically understand who Maria was or why she had come to me in this way. My mind wasn't prepared to accept data of this type, or to interpret an experience so far outside the boundaries of normalcy. I sat looking at the statue of Mary to the right of the altar, trying to bridge the gap between the Lady I had prayed to all my life and the young vibrant woman I met on the hill. Were they the same, or was it time to release the childish icons of my youth?

I sat through two services that evening, one in Croatian and the other in English. I went to communion both times, and it felt as if I was taking Maria into my body. The sensual feeling that swept through me was astounding, as if she was pouring her love into my mouth and it filled my entire being. There were no words to describe what I felt, only the high, glorious chant of, "Maria, Maria, Maria." It resounded in my ears and resonated in my soul. The infatuation that began when I met her in the streets of Belgrade had blossomed into an all-encompassing love, a passionate crescendo the likes of which I had never experienced before.

When it was time to lock up the church I left and returned to my room. I don't know how long I lay there waiting for sleep, for it was as if I was in a dream already. The whole day was a remarkable blur of light and love, and I imagined what it would be like to be with her again, to feel her presence and to sense her radiance. She had become the Beloved, the sacred lover leading to a Divine ocean, not the mother I had known before. Where had that woman gone? Was she capable of being both to me, moving back and forth like a ghost or an apparition? She was no apparition, of this I was sure. The woman I met on the hill in Medjugorje was solid and real, and I was in love with her. Even if she returned the next day in a form I was not prepared for, returning to the traditional image I was raised to adore, her essence would have been captured in my mind and in my soul. She would always be there waiting for me.

 awoke at dawn and prepared to return to the hill. Maria never said what time we would meet again, and as far as I was concerned it didn't matter at all. Even if I had to wait on the hill all day, till the sun fell behind the horizon and the stars began their evening dance, that was better than anything else I knew. At least I would be in the place where she came to me, that holy spot where she had destroyed my former self. That's how it felt to me, that a part of me had suddenly died and was replaced by something completely new. Would it last, this new life she gave? Such thoughts were so far away at that moment. All I could focus on was our next meeting, and the sudden fix of her gaze.

On the way to the hill I felt a strong impulse to go inside one of the many tourist shops that lined the narrow road. As I walked around the small store my eye caught a pile of disposable cameras, and it felt as though I heard a voice telling me to buy one. It had been years since I had owned a camera, and I was tempted to ignore the direction. But then it became stronger, and more insistent. "Buy the camera," it said with conviction. It seemed that I didn't have a choice. I paid the woman at the counter and placed it in my jacket pocket.

The path up the hill was deserted and I climbed to the spot where I had left the path the day before. The thorns and rocks were nothing to me that morning, and I glided over every obstacle that formerly would have slowed my pace. How long had it been since I felt this energy, this rush of adrenaline and life, catapulting through my heart with piercing accuracy? Was I really in love, I asked myself? Be careful… don't lose yourself to the aroma of her presence. Remember who this is, no matter how she appears… no matter how she appears. It's true, she fills the emptiness as only a goddess can… but remember who sits behind those eyes, the Divine

Mother… the feminine principle itself. Don't jump off the cliff holding onto the apparition of an angel.

Minutes later I could see the peace pole in the distance, and my heart leapt for joy when I saw her sitting next to it, waiting for me.

"Good morning," she said as she moved over on the rock where she sat, making room for me to sit next to her. I felt my mind begin to slow its sudden pace as I approached her side. The hectic anticipation of the climb was gone, and my heart began to swim in an ocean of peace.

"I didn't know if you would be here yet," I said to her as I sat down. "I knew I had to come as soon as I could. I couldn't wait any longer."

"I have waited for you longer than you know," she said. "And you have waited for me as well, haven't you?"

I didn't answer for a moment. I wasn't sure what she meant, though my heart moved with recognition. "I have waited for you… in many ways, I'm sure. All I know is that the moment you approached me on this hill… no, the moment I saw you in Belgrade, my heart came alive. It's like waking up from a dream — I didn't realize I was asleep until now."

"And yet there's more, isn't there?" Her blue, radiant eyes sparkled wildly when she said these words, as if she was reminding me of something I had forgotten, but which was extremely important. She waited for me to make the next move.

"I'm not sure I know what you mean," I said.

"When you were with the Emissaries you had no way of knowing who they were or what they were really doing. Therefore, there was no way for you to understand why you were the one that was brought to them. Haven't you wondered about that? The Emissaries of Light have been praying for the enlightenment of humanity for two thousand years, and yet when it came time to end their mission they came to you. Why?"

"I never found out," I said to her. "I figured it was because I was there… available. I never read much more into it than that."

"But there is more," she said. "A great deal more. And you've already begun to remember. You've begun to understand who the Emissaries really are."

"You mean the 'Community of the Beloved Disciple,' don't you? So it is true. The Emissaries come from the lineage of St. John. When the church began persecuting the order they went underground and have remained there ever since. That means that St. John's role has been fulfilled. Jesus said that John would remain until he came again, or at least his community would. The fact that the Emissaries have disbanded must mean that he has returned. John himself is not here to witness it, but the community he started is."

"No, he meant what he said," Maria said to me. "John has remained, and is here right now."

"I don't understand," I said. "Do you mean reincarnation?"

"The idea you have of reincarnation is a fantasy," she said to me. "The truth is much simpler than you expect... and more complicated, depending upon how you look at it. John never left the earth, and neither did Jesus."

"Are you saying that they've been on earth for the last two thousand years? But how is that possible?"

"You believe that this realm is limited to the physical world you perceive," she said. "There are many other levels of reality you have yet to perceive, and they are just as real as this one. It is from these deeper levels that the essential work has taken place. It was to this realm that Jesus ascended after his resurrection, and it is there that he has remained, along with John and many others, waiting for the time of the great shift. You can consider them a group of overseers, kind of a board of directors.

"The Emissaries were the physical counterpart of this unique group, made up of beings who have achieved mastery on this level of existence, from every religion and spiritual path. There are other levels of reality beyond the one where John and Jesus work, what you might call the angelic realms. The Emissaries were like an anchor point that served as a physical link between all these etheric planes and the physical world."

"We've always been taught that Jesus ascended into Heaven," I said to her, "and I would expect St. John to be there as well. It sounds like you're saying that they're somewhere in-between, and that they will someday leave that realm and return to earth."

Maria smiled when I said these words, a loving smile, but the kind one gives a child when they don't understand. "You can call it Heaven if you want. In many ways it is very similar to your concept of Heaven. And yet there is so much more, many other levels that are so subtle you have no way of understanding them. The masters do not return from these levels physically, unless it's in a form like the one you're perceiving right now. I have assumed this body in order to teach you a particular lesson. When the lesson is over the body is gone.

"What returns to the world is what you might call an 'energetic signature.' For example, 'The Christ' is an experience, not a person. Please understand this because it is of vital importance — Jesus was certainly the Christ, but the Christ is not limited to your idea of who Jesus was. Jesus assumed that frame of reference, or that energetic signature, and therefore became the savior of his age. The teacher you are waiting for, what you call the 'next teacher', will assume the same frame of reference as Jesus. It will be the same, and yet it will be different. It will be Jesus, but it will be more."

"I'm not sure if I understand," I said. "What about the Second Coming? Does Jesus ever come back to earth, or is it his soul that returns?"

"It is both, and it is neither," she said. "I'm sorry that it doesn't make logical sense, but there's no way to understand it logically. Jesus, beyond his body and personality, has always been present on the etheric levels waiting to return to earth. This is the predestined time of awakening, the moment when 'The Christ' returns to initiate the New World. But it will not happen the way you think. In other words, don't expect a Jewish man with a beard to appear and save the world. And that brings us back to John and the society he founded.

"Before Jesus died on the cross he put me, his mother, in the care of John," she continued. "From that day on I was cared for by the apostle as well as the disciples that followed him. He was with me when I was assumed into the real world, and many years later he followed the same path. He did not die a physical death as is believed. He has continued as a living master to the community he founded, and most importantly, has protected the greatest mystery of all — the very nature of Christ's return. You see, there are actually two manifestations of the Christ energy. For the last two thousand years Jesus, in his identity as the masculine Christ, has personified that manifestation. The New World I spoke of is essentially a shifting of poles. The energy of the Christ, just as everything must, is about to find balance."

"I'm still not following this," I said to her frustrated. "Shrinat Devi said something similar — that there is another Christ... but what does this have to do with St. John?"

"For two thousand years John has cared for and protected what you're calling the 'next teacher,'" she said. "He took her into his home and into his heart... and is now bringing her back to the world."

"But you said that you're not the one I've been waiting for," I said, "and yet you are the one he cared for. Doesn't that mean you're the 'next teacher'?"

"No, but the energy I carry is," she said to me. "Look past your idea of who you think I am, past this appearance or the way you were raised to believe in me. It is the feminine nature of God that I bring, the energy of compassion and peace. John's role was not only to protect that energy, but to give it back to the world. And that is what John is now doing — through you."

"What? Now I'm really lost."

"Let me explain this in another way," she said. "As you have already suspected, before he ascended Jesus realized that there would be a separation between the institutional church headed by Peter, and the inner church headed by John. It is also clear from the gospel that Peter did not understand John's role; and how could he when his primary responsibility was to organize and establish what would become a strong institution? While Peter and the others were out preaching and establishing the Church, John was engrossed in the ecstatic visions that became the 'Book of Revelations.' He and his disciples were developing their understanding of the esoteric realities which were the key to Jesus' mystical spirituality... the secrets of the resurrection and ascension, the healing of the sick and the raising of the dead.

"Now, the Roman Catholic Church has always taught that the pope is the successor of St. Peter, the first pope. It also teaches that a sacred relationship is established each time a new pope takes office, and that the new leader acts 'as Peter.' This is the true meaning of papal infallibility. It has nothing to do with reincarnation, but everything to do with 'energetic signature.' The pope actually enters an energy field that was once occupied by the apostle himself. Whether or not the new pope accepts and activates that energy field is another question, but it is there nonetheless.

"The same has been true of the inner church as well," she said. "Since the ascension of John there have been hundreds of people who have stepped into the energy field he left behind, just as the pope steps into the energy field left behind by St. Peter. Each one of them has continued the sacred task of holding the 'feminine Christ' in their heart, guarding and loving that light until the time would come for it to be activated. They have acted 'as John,' and have carried out the mission given to John. When the church became so afraid of this lineage that it tried to have it destroyed, the most secret branch of the order went underground to preserve the mission. They have been known by many names, the Cathars, the Knights Templar, the Bogomils, and most recently as the Emissaries of Light. They have existed for two thousand years, and it has not come to an end, only shifted direction."

"If what you say is true about the pope, then the same must be true of Teacher, the focus of the Emissaries. Was he the one who carried the lineage back to John?"

"That's correct," she said. "And now that he is gone he has passed it on to another. And that person is you, Jimmy."

I nearly gasped when she said this, and yet I could feel the direction where she was leading me. I had wondered why the Emissaries had entrusted me with their message for the last three years. People often asked me the same question and I always felt embarrassed to be set apart, to seem special in some way. I am definitely not special, I often said to them, and that's why I was chosen, because it's time for all of us to step into the experience the Emissaries spoke of. But what Maria said was very different. She seemed to be saying that I was special, as if I had some unique gift to offer.

"It is not that you are special," she said, reading my thoughts. "It has nothing to do with being special, so get over that right away. Each one of us comes into the world possessing unique gifts, and it is our responsibility to use these gifts wisely and for the betterment of humanity. It is like a play with many characters and costumes. Each character has specific lines to perform, and they are expected to perform them convincingly. Some actors have more lines than other actors, but that doesn't make them more important. When the play is over and the curtains fall, they are the same again. When the costumes come off and the makeup is removed, they are no different than any other person."

"But why me?" I asked. "Who am I to be given such a role?"

"All I can say is that you chose it a very long time ago. Think of it as a contract you made before you were born. It's time for you to honor your end of the deal."

She smiled when she said these words. It was obviously a joke, but I wasn't laughing. And yet there was a part of me, a very deep part, that knew what she said was true. In a way it didn't surprise me at all. There were many people in the world, very ordinary people, who were waking up to extraordinary missions, and I knew that. One I knew personally was Nick Bunick, the subject of the book, *The Messengers*. I had met and become friends with Nick through the speaking circuit, and though I was at first a bit suspicious of his claims to be the reincarnation of St. Paul, our friendship had convinced me otherwise. It was clear to me that Nick had an important mission to fulfill, but anyone who had known him up until that particular time in his life would have never expected such grandeur.

The same was true for me... even I wouldn't have suspected this revelation. And yet on some level, in some way, it was true, and I knew it.

"What does it all mean?" I asked her. "What do you want me to do?"

"You are already doing it," she said to me as she touched my arm. The feel of her slight tender fingers against my skin sent amazing vibrations through my body. I wanted her to hold the contact, but she removed her hand a few seconds later. "You have been extending the message of the Emissaries exactly as you were asked. But now you have come to the next phase. Do you remember when Teacher told you to initiate the next group of Emissaries? Now that the inner community has externalized, now that the Emissaries are out, it's time for you to begin this next stage, that of calling the Community of the Beloved Disciple back together. You see, I want you to reconcile Peter and John."

I couldn't believe my ears. Could she possibly have meant what I thought? If she did, then I knew I was in over my head. She was asking me to help her bridge the ancient schism that had formed between the institutional church and the inner church founded by St. John. The Catholic Church had persecuted this lineage, and was it not now time to lay all differences aside? But this would sound like folly to anyone outside the narrow esoteric circle where I traveled. No card-carrying Sunday-going churchgoer would listen to such nonsense.

"How could I do such a thing?" I asked her. "Who am I... "

"It has nothing to do with you, Jimmy," she said. "It has to do with me... with the essence of the feminine Christ. This is the time ordained for healing and reunion. They are like two estranged brothers who were forced apart. One gained the kingdom and the other was forced into the netherlands. But times have changed, as you have seen. If humanity is going to finally create the world of peace you have envisioned, then it has to be done together — the inner and the outer church as one body. This is what a mother does, she brings her beloved children together in reconciliation."

"But why is this so focused on Christianity?" I asked. "What about all the other faiths?"

"You ask this question because you are of the lineage of the Beloved Disciple," she said. "This was one of the most important teachings of Jesus, adopted by the inner church and ignored until now by the institution. Every path to God is the same when it is centered on love and compassion. It has nothing to do with accepting a particular personality or savior. The only savior is love itself. St. John learned this from Jesus, but the outer church has only just now laid aside the barriers that have kept it isolated from the beauty of every other tradition. The people you will initiate, along with all those who are already working for the goal I give, will preach this gospel, and the feminine Christ will then be revealed."

"Once again, I must ask this... Are you the feminine Christ?"

"I carry the feminine Christ in my heart," she said. "And because my heart is open, you sense only that Light. But each one of us carries that same Light, though it has been blocked by centuries of fear and distrust. But the time of awakening is at hand, and you have all been impregnated with the Light of all lights. As you move closer to the appointed moment, Light will grow within you, until you come to the end of your waiting. Then the Light will be born and will come into the world again. When I say you, I mean all of you, for the Feminine Christ comes not through one, but through all. This is the message of the Beloved Disciple, and it is now your message."

"You said that I have been given the authority left behind by St. John," I said. "What am I meant to do with that authority?"

"It would be best that you don't use the word 'authority,'" she said to me. "It is an ignorant world since it doesn't allow for the true meaning of leadership. You have no more authority than anyone else, but you, as well as several others, do carry the mantle left behind by the apostle. He was the one charged with watching over the feminine Christ, caring for my needs. The other members of the order, both those who were with John as well as those who came after him, were charged with the same task. When I left the physical plane, that task did not change but was internalized. This was one of the great mysteries of the Community of the Beloved Disciple — that of holding the feminine Christ in the most sacred chamber of their hearts until the time would come for its release in the world."

"And that time has come now?" I asked.

"Indeed, it has come now," she said with a smile that lit up the whole world. "That is why the Emissary role has shifted to you, and to those who are with you. It is time for the reemergence of the feminine Christ, the compassion of God which has always been present in the world but which has slept beneath the blanket of illusion. The mission of John's order is to reveal its nature, and the time has come for that to happen. You have experienced for yourself the mystery of the Emissaries, and now it's time for the whole world to experience it."

"Maria," I said to her, my head pounding from everything I had heard. "You have to know how afraid I am… perhaps not afraid, but confused. I have always known these things somewhere in the back of my mind, but I tried to force them away. When I was a child I sensed this revelation, but I had no way of understanding it, so I turned it into a vain, impossible dream. But it wasn't a dream, was it? You were the one who was talking to me, weren't you? It was your voice I heard."

"As I said before, I have always been with you. We are together now, but we have been together before. Do you remember?"

"What do you mean?" I asked. "We've been together in another time?"

"It doesn't matter now. It will come to you when you are ready. But there is one thing you need to know now. There are those who would try and stop your mission. You have already encountered these forces, and they are determined to disrupt what has begun to take root. I want you to be aware of this, and that is all. You will know what to do when the time is right."

"You're right, I have already felt it. I had to overcome enormous obstacles to get here, as if they wanted me to stay away."

"They did," she said. "It was essential that we meet here in Medjugorje, and now we are ready to take the next step. You will have to undergo many trials before we meet again, but remember that I am with you. Once this journey begins, its end is sure."

Then I asked her something that surprised us both. I reached into my jacket pocket and touched the camera. "Maria, I know this will sound strange, and I can't believe I'm going to ask you this… but do you mind if I take a picture of you?" I held my breath for a long moment while she looked at me.

"Not at all," she finally said. "If you believe it will help you, take my picture."

I could feel my legs flex as my body rose from the rock, and that was all I felt. It was as if I was in a dream, and I couldn't relate to what was really happening. She sat there on the rock and I stood back from her. Her smile was subtle and her eyes shone bright. I took one shot… it was all I dared to take.

Then she stood up and stepped back from me. It felt as if my skin was being torn away from me, as if we had merged and had become one being. The last few words she spoke scared me and I didn't want her to leave. I didn't want to be alone again.

"Do not tell anyone these things for now," she said. "You must wait for the drama to play itself out, then you will understand. Just know that the Light has come into the world, and the night is nearly over."

She turned around and started walking up the hill. I couldn't move or say a word. By then the sun was bright and I could hear the sound of pilgrims walking up the hill in the distance. "If they only knew," I said to myself. But how could they? They wouldn't recognize her even if she walked up the hill beside them. And that was the way it should be, for that was the essence of her words to me. It's time to find God in the ordinary — in each other. It was my mission, as well as the mission of the ancient Community. It was out in the open now — they were out in the open. How could I have predicted all this?

"I love you so much," she said as she turned toward me again. And yet the words were not heard by my ears, but with my heart. It was the voice from my childhood, the beautiful voice of God that had thrilled and confused me so. "You will know what to do, for I will tell you everything. Trust me, and realize how much I trust you."

Then she walked away, disappearing over the hill.

I wish I could remember and write down every word Maria said to me in Medjugorje. I do know the simple dialogue I've recorded here contains the essence of her message, and that is what's important. The energy of her presence fills me still and is with me constantly. That visit did change my life, and I am forever indebted to her for not forgetting a promise I made a very long time ago.

 week later I was back at Liz Story's house in Prescott, Arizona. I had been traveling for nearly a month and was happy to have time to focus on everything that had happened. The sky was filled with millions of stars, entire clouds of possible worlds. And that was when I saw it — the comet. At first it didn't dawn on me that there was any particular significance to it, but then I remembered her words: "The whole world will see me flash through the sky with a tail of light. Then you'll know it has begun."

Hale-Bopp was more than an astronomical phenomenon; it was a sign from Heaven, a promise that everything is going according to plan.

Part Two

he art community in Mexico began paying attention to Jacqueline Ripstein when she was twelve years old. Although she had no formal training as an artist, they knew there was something special about her. She won a national competition that year, and though her skill was still unformed, there was magic in her strokes, and they all knew it. A love affair had begun — Jacqueline's love of art and art's love of Jacqueline.

She moved to Florida in 1994, four years after her husband was brutally murdered in the family's garage in Mexico City. A long period of questioning began, questions about her life and her art. "There must be more," she thought to herself. "My life has to have a purpose, not just fame, but a higher calling." Jacqueline was already a well-known and respected artist in Mexico, but the US was a new and open territory. She made a commitment to herself to take her work to a new level, to become an instrument of truth and unconditional universal love.

"God sometimes plays tricks on us," she would later say. "We think we are asking for one thing, but then we're given something completely different, something we never would have expected. It's our job to open ourselves to God and be willing to give everything — our talent, our energy. Then we can be truly used, because we will not be deciding the moves ourselves. It will be God working through us."

In March, 1997, the same month that I was invited to Belgrade, Jacqueline was commissioned by Diana Abouzeid to paint Mary, the Mother of Jesus, for a renewal center in Bosnia. Diana had founded the center to help families and children living near Medjugorje who were affected by the war between the Croats, Muslims and Serbs. The renewal center would be a safe haven, a place where people of every religion could receive love, compassion and hope. Jacqueline immediately felt connected with the project, but wondered if it were really appropriate for her to paint Our Lady. As an artist she had learned to embrace all religions, and to see the ways they were the same, not separate. But she had been raised Jewish, and despite her understanding that Mary transcends religious and ethnic barriers, she still felt slightly apprehensive about the way the churches would act toward her. Diana's unconditional love and support helped Jacqueline face and transcend her tests and fears. It was a reminder of the Universality of Our Lady's message, the love of a mother that would unite humanity.

"Our Lady's message to the children in Medjugorje is universal," Diana told her. "In one of the apparitions the children asked her who was the most devout in the whole area, and she named a young girl whom they all knew. The children were confused because the girl was not Catholic, but Muslim. 'But you didn't ask who was the most devout Catholic,' Mary explained. 'Devotion has nothing to do with religion.'"

"I understand what you are saying," Jacqueline said. "As an artist I appreciate the importance of being open to the truths found in all religions. But shouldn't I have a special connection to Our Lady? Don't you want an artist who is deeply connected to her?"

"If you are the one whom she wants to paint this picture, then she'll let you know in one way or another. I am going on a pilgrimage to Medjugorje in a few weeks. Why don't you join us? Then you'll discover for yourself how deep your connection is."

Jacqueline accepted the invitation and began preparing for the journey. Within days she found herself beginning a three-month fast. She felt compelled to purify her body, spirit and mind for the first time in her twenty-six year career, not knowing why. For several weeks she prayed and meditated, asking to be shown the next step. A decision was made not to accept the commission unless it was clearly the will of Mary. Though Jacqueline had accepted many offers to paint spiritual themes, she knew that this request was unique. The message would have to be unmistakable and her own conviction absolute; otherwise she would decline the offer.

The trip to Medjugorje played a pivotal role in the evolution of the painting and Jacqueline's own spiritual journey. The group arrived in Bosnia and was overwhelmed not only by the incredible spiritual energy that defines this region, but also by the violence that has strangled it for centuries. While Medjugorje itself stands as a symbol of peace and tolerance, Mostar, one of the worst examples of injustice and hatred, is only a few miles away. It was here that the Croatian Catholics massacred hundreds of Muslims, destroying their homes and the bridge that had for centuries stood as a monument for peace. It seemed appropriate that Mary would pick this place to bring a message of hope, this region of Bosnia that seemed to have none.

One of the members of the pilgrimage was a Catholic priest named Father Thomas. During the bus trip from Zagreb to Medjugorje he decided to satisfy his own curiosity about the woman who was asked to paint the Blessed Mother. He had doubts about Diana's decision to commission Jacqueline. He would have preferred a Catholic, or at least a Christian, for such a sacred task. He moved to the back of the bus as soon as he was able, and asked if he could sit down next to her.

"How do you feel about this commission?" he asked Jacqueline. "I'm sure you realize it is a great honor to be asked to paint Our Lady. There are those who will wonder why a Jewish woman was chosen."

"I wish I knew why I was chosen, Father. But I don't believe that one's religion should be considered a limitation. Whether I am Jewish, or Christian, or Hindu... what matters is my willingness to follow God's will."

"Is it possible for us to know God's will?" he asked. "Surely you have your own reasons for accepting this job, and they may or may not be Divinely inspired."

"The fact that I have been asked to do it says enough. I did not ask for this. Diana came to me. And I still do not know if I will accept. That is why I am on this trip with you, to discern the will of God."

"Do you believe in Jesus?"

Jacqueline was shocked by the abruptness of his question.

"Do you believe in God?" she asked him.

"Of course I do. How could I be a priest if... "

"Then you believe that the will of God is beyond what either one of us can fathom," she said. "Therefore, how can any of us make a judgment about what we think is appropriate or inappropriate. It is not our place. All we can do is support each other in our desire to know God's will for ourselves. And that is what I am doing, Father. I know that you only want what is best for this project, and in this we are the same. All I ask is that you pray for Our Lady to show me my mission."

Father Thomas returned to his seat, his expression an odd mixture of humility and outrage. Jacqueline knew that he would keep his eye on her, and if he thought it necessary, he would make his displeasure public. She knew that she made him uncomfortable. If she was not the one to paint Mary, then she hoped she would feel it. But if she were, then what?

Medjugorje was nothing like Jacqueline expected. The once small village was now overflowing with tourist shops, each one trying to profit from the constant influx of tourists willing to stock up on ceramic statues and plastic rosaries. The commercialism disturbed her. Was this what faith was all about? She made her way through the streets, wondering. It wasn't until she left the busy main street and headed toward the Hill of the Apparition that she finally felt the real energy of Medjugorje.

Groups of pilgrims walked along the worn, narrow path that led up the hill, some praying and others chatting quietly to one another. There was a reverence she sensed on that long climb that spoke more about the meaning of Our Lady's message than anything else. Her convictions told her that this hill was the place to do her own praying — a heartfelt request that she be shown what to do. She knew that it was the true heart of the village, the place where the visitations began. This was where she would get her answer.

Something or someone on the hill seemed to be watching her — a warm, beautiful presence that filled her with incredible joy. It was as if the ground itself had absorbed Our Lady's Light and was radiating a blessing. Or was it more? Maybe she was not alone. Of course there were people all around her, but that's not what the feeling was. It was so intense, like a laser beam of such intensity that it seared her heart, opening it completely. What was happening, she wondered.

When she got back to the bottom of the hill, she stopped at a small chapel that had a statue of Mary in the courtyard. It too seemed to glow with the same energy she had felt on the hill. The feeling of being watched by something Divine returned, but she turned, thinking it was her imagination, and began walking to the village.

Late in the afternoon of the first day, Diana informed the group that they would soon be meeting Father Jozo Zovko, the spiritual leader of Medjugorje. It was Father Jozo who had been thrown into prison and tortured because he did not put an end to the Medjugorje children's 'ridiculous claims.' The local authorities had been undeniably nervous over the devotion the apparitions were inspiring. Revolution was in the air, and they didn't want it fanned by the fervor of religious fanaticism. Since his release, Father Jozo had been in constant demand. And yet this humble Franciscan was not at all interested in the fame he was acquiring, and the chance to meet him was a rare honor.

Diana introduced the priest to Jacqueline as soon as they arrived at the center where he worked. He had already heard about the proposed commission and was curious to meet the Jewish woman chosen to paint Mary. Father Jozo did not immediately question the choice because of her religious background. His openness was testimony of an extraordinary human being who looks past boundaries and is connected to the oneness of all. He believed that as long as Jacqueline came to understand Mary and her message, her painting would be perfect. Jacqueline was immediately taken with the angelic priest and was happy when some days later he invited her to accompany him to visit a group of widows from the war.

The room was hot and crowded when they arrived. The women were bunched together at a long table, sewing small items that would later be sold in the village. Father Jozo asked Jacqueline to sit down at the head of the table, and through the aid of a translator, invited her to talk with the women.

"We find strength in each other," one woman said. "It is good to be with other people who understand how we feel."

"Our sorrow has been great," murmured an older woman who was bent over the table. "But there are thousands of women like us in Bosnia, wives and mothers, all who have lost their families to this terrible war."

Jacqueline was incredibly moved by their openness and honesty. Their willingness to sit down with someone from another country, someone they had never met and who could never truly understand their problems, helped to bring her closer to making a decision about her commission.

After listening to their stories, Jacqueline spoke, keeping the pace of her words slow to allow the translator to keep up. "I am not so different from you," she said. "Your war was obvious... in the open. The horror was there for all to see. I come from a place where the war is hidden, locked away so the world can't see it. Many women in Mexico feel the same sadness as you. My own husband was shot dead getting into his car, standing in his own garage. We never found out who killed him, and it took me many years to forgive them. That's why it's so important for me to be with you here, to see that we are the same. Your pain is my pain, and I'm here with you today to help in any way I can."

As they left the room Father Jozo touched Jacqueline's arm. "Thank you for what you said in there. I believe you have been chosen for this job... to paint Our Lady. It takes someone like you to understand her compassion. And that is what you will paint, not a woman but her essence. People may not see her with their eyes, but will feel her with their hearts. I am honored that you have accepted this role."

Had she already accepted? Father Jozo was so certain, and his confidence was contagious. For the first time Jacqueline felt that she might accept. She began to believe that perhaps there were important reasons she had been asked, reasons she didn't understand. Her reluctance seemed to be disappearing, replaced by a certainty that made her feel strong.

The next morning the entire group met at St. James' Church in the center of Medjugorje. Jacqueline sat in the second row with several of her new friends, observing the diverse crowd. She was moved by the sincerity of these people, pilgrims from all over the world who had come to absorb just a hint of the mystery that surrounded and permeated this place.

But what did they want and why were they really there? Was it to have their own vision, or to simply be close to the vortex of Medjugorje? Jacqueline felt an overpowering sense of love for everyone she saw. She was beginning to feel the real energy of this holy site, not so much the residual of Mary's presence which floated above them like the scent of flowers, but the love and commitment brought by the people themselves. This was the real magic, and the transformation they experienced was their own.

Jacqueline's attention began to wander during the mass. She was looking around the church, lost in her thoughts, when something caught the corner of her eye. She looked above the altar and to the left, straight into the light that came in through one of the stained glass windows. What she saw reflected in the sun defied explanation, and she knew exactly what it meant. A beautiful woman floated in the light, looking down with incredible love and grace at the crowd. Jacqueline's face must have changed dramatically, because others began to look in the same direction and see the same thing.

"It's her," someone nearby whispered in awe. "You can see Our Lady in the light."

Others said it was a simply an optical illusion, a trick of the light, but for Jacqueline it was a sign — a sign from Heaven that put her mind at ease. She wondered how she would ever be able to capture the beauty of this magnificent woman. Mere paint could never capture what she had seen, but she felt she would try. If it was Mary's will that this painting be done, then she would have to guide the brush in Jacqueline's hand. Otherwise it would be just another face, another image on another canvas.

Jacqueline returned to Florida and immediately set about the task of completing her commission. She was surprised to feel that familiar doubt, the apprehension which she thought the trip to Medjugorje had cured.

Everything seemed to be pointing her toward the work but a feeling of inadequacy persisted, as if there were still a part of her, however small, which did not believe all the signs, all the ways Heaven was moving her heart toward Mary.

Four days later she stood in front of an empty canvas waiting for inspiration. The sketch pad she carried with her was filled with ideas, faces and figures that could develop into a living work of art. But some block was keeping her at arms length, just beyond the reach of the image she longed for. There was, however, one idea that kept surfacing over and over. She saw Mary floating on a cloud with the Earth far below. Jacqueline could see Mary's face in her mind's eye, but she didn't know if it would work when set to canvas.

Jacqueline struggled all day with these strong emotional tests, making the task of painting Our Lady even harder. Then she opened the Bible to the Book of Job, to a passage that led her to believe that the tests were there for a reason. She realized that the stronger the pain and the lesson, the more powerful the opportunity. She decided to transcend the negativity and sat down to begin sketching Our Lady. She would continue on, but she still needed help. Where would the help come from, she wondered.

It was nearly ten-thirty at night, and Jacqueline was tired. She had been struggling with the sketch all day and needed to set it aside. Before she did, she took the pad to a small altar she had set up in her studio. There was a tall, clear, glass vigil candle burning there, and she set the pad beside it. Jacqueline asked for another sign, one more intervention to put her mind to rest. Was this the image that Mary wanted, the one she had been sketching all day long? If it was, if she was on the right track, then she needed confirmation. She asked Mary to show her what to do next. She was perfectly willing to call the whole project off, or to move forward. But she needed direct knowledge, otherwise she would do nothing.

Jacqueline woke up an hour and a half later, at exactly midnight, to the wailing sound of one of the condominium's fire alarms. She threw on her robe and ran to the dining room. There was no smoke or sign of a fire, and she immediately noticed that the only activated alarm was just outside her bedroom door. Attempts to turn it off failed, so a maintenance man came to give assistance. There was nothing he could do but dismantle the unit, then take it to the shop to be worked on the next day.

On her way back into the bedroom, Jacqueline passed the altar with the candle and the pad. Something about the candle stopped her in her tracks. It had been burning for three days and was clear all that time. But now there seemed to be an object glowing in the light, as if the wax had formed an image on the inside of the glass. What she saw in that moment was the final straw, the miracle that convinced her that she had indeed been chosen to paint Our Lady. The wax had formed in the exact image she had sketched on the pad earlier that day. Jacqueline opened the pad to compare the images, make sure she wasn't crazy, and there it was, line for line, identical in every respect. As she looked again at the wax image, the candle light shining through it made it seem alive, gave the illusion of movement. Tears trickled down her cheeks. Her prayer had been answered... again.

She picked up the pad and immediately went to the studio. She painted for hours that night, taking full advantage of the Divine energy she felt all around her. By morning the image was already coming to life, and every doubt she had felt so strongly before was completely gone.

Several days later, Jacqueline invited a friend to her home to see the vigil candle and the image of Mary. The woman was overcome with joy by the miracle and left the apartment filled with wonder hours later. When she stepped off the elevator at the ground floor, she nearly ran into an elderly gentleman who was walking past. She braced herself by grabbing his arm, then apologized for not looking where she was going. The man gazed directly into her eyes and immediately sensed something unusual about her presence.

"There is a glow in your eyes that is beautiful," he said to her. "You must have just had a wonderful experience."

"You might say that I've just witnessed a miracle," she told him.

"You have been visiting someone here in this building?"

"Yes, my friend is an artist and... "

"I must meet your friend," he said with urgency. "I do not know why but I feel it's important. I am a rabbi and I promise I will not bother her."

"My friend is also Jewish, but I'm sorry, I can't give you her name. That would be intruding on her privacy."

The rabbi continued to insist that he meet Jacqueline, but the woman refused and left. Convinced that his intuition was correct, the man began to ask questions of other residents until he discovered Jacqueline's name, the only artist in the building. He left a message for Jacqueline with security and she called him the next day.

"I am glad you came," Jacqueline said over the phone, and then she explained the miracle of the candle. "Some wax markings have appeared on the glass above the image, and they look like Hebrew letters. Unfortunately I cannot speak Hebrew, so perhaps you can tell me what they mean."

The rabbi came to her home later that day. Jacqueline opened the door and saw a small elderly man with a black coat and yamulkah on the crown of his head, his eyes narrow and intense. She invited him into the living room where several other friends waited. They chatted for a few moments until she brought in the candle. The old man examined it for several minutes, holding it up to the light to determine for himself if it was truly authentic. When he was satisfied, he set it down and looked across the table at Jacqueline.

"There are two things I must tell you," he said. "The first is that they are not only Hebrew letters, but actual words."

"What are the words, Rabbi?" she asked, almost trembling inside.

"They say, 'God exists and makes miracles.'"

Jacqueline was stunned. It was hard to believe that her story could get any more fantastic. If she were not a part of it, she doubted she would believe it at all. Taking a deep breath, she asked, "What is the other thing you must tell me?"

"This miracle may come from God, but you must turn away from these people." His voice had suddenly grown cold and it cut through her. The look on his face could not be described, and she pulled her hand away when he leaned over the table to touch her.

"Dear child, you have fallen into a trap... They have brainwashed you," he said, his voice trembling a bit. "You are Jewish, not Christian. These words are a sign from God to turn back to your blood. Why else would they appear in Hebrew?"

"As a artist I have no religion," she said. "And yet everything that has happened to me has been from God. Maybe it's because Mary herself was Jewish."

"Please listen to me," he said in a gentle, concerned voice. "I know how fantastic this miracle seems, and I agree that it is something to consider. But this woman you have painted is a Christian, not a Jew. You cannot devote yourself to her, or this painting, or even this miracle, and still consider yourself Jewish."

Jacqueline recognized something in his eyes that she had seen before. It was the same fear she had glimpsed in the eyes of Father Thomas. Both men were afraid of being wrong. For Father Thomas, a Jewish woman being chosen to paint Mary threatened his idea that Catholicism was the only true church. For the rabbi, it meant that authentic miracles could actually occur beyond his strict adherence to Judaism. These two men were actually very much alike, Jacqueline realized. And because everything we ever do is either an act of love or a call for love, she decided to look past his attack and give him what he really needed.

"I am sorry that you feel this way," she said to him. "But there is only one way I have of determining what is or is not from God. It is love. Everything that has happened around my accepting this commission has been loving. And now this miracle has happened, and it tells me to follow that love." As Jacqueline said this, she kept hearing the words in her mind, "God exists and makes miracles."

"Then why do you need me?" the rabbi asked.

"You were sent to tell me what the letters meant," Jacqueline said. "And that is how I know to follow through with this painting. Please try to understand, I don't want to turn against anything you believe in. But I think we all have an incredible opportunity here, to see past the ways we are different to the ways we are the same. It may take a miracle for this to happen, and here it is."

"I am inspired by your conviction," he said, "and I will take all these things to prayer. Maybe I am too old to understand these things… maybe you are right. I cannot deny this miracle, and I will try to let go of my judgments."

Minutes later the rabbi excused himself and left the apartment. Jacqueline sat down on the couch and looked at the candle again. She felt a warm sensation as if the candle was still lit, and she knew that it was a spiritual light that burned within her. Institutional and dogmatic religions were trying to distance themselves from her experience, and she knew it wouldn't work. The energy was too strong, and the miracles were too important to deny. It actually seemed to fit in with everything she felt about Mary. "She has come to bring about radical compassion and forgiveness," Jacqueline thought, "not judgment. It is her desire to unite people, not separate them further. Maybe this was what it took, this strange polarization as a first step."

The new energy that Jacqueline felt inspired her to throw herself into the painting. She found that she had entered an amazing artistic flow, her hand sweeping over the canvas with a strange agility and grace. A short time later there was only one thing missing — the eyes. For some reason Jacqueline discovered she couldn't focus on this last detail, for it would give the painting life, and there was something odd about that feeling. It was like the hesitancy a mother may feel during the conclusion of her birth labor, moments before bringing a child into the world. But by then it is too late, for the child is already formed and needs only to breathe. Our Lady of the Universe, the painting Jacqueline was commissioned to birth, was waiting to take its first breath.

She went to a respected healer four times, hoping it would help her overcome this final barrier. Each time she came back to her studio and stood in front of the painting waiting for something to happen. It wouldn't breathe, she thought. She was afraid to let it breathe. But then she went for one final visit to the healer, one last chance to break into the light.

As she lay on the table, she could feel an amazing energy rush through her body. It was as if a brilliant beam of light had penetrated her soul, intimately linking itself to the most essential part of her life. There was a gentle rhythm to the experience, as if it was rocking within her. At first she was afraid and wanted it to go away, but it was so gentle, so persistent that she decided to wait, just for a moment, to see where it would lead. Then she saw the eyes in her mind, as if Our Lady were looking straight through her. She still didn't move, but lay motionless on the table for one last moment. Then it was over, but she felt something shift, or perhaps fall away.

hen she returned to the studio, she went to the painting and instinctively picking up the brush, she began to paint the eyes, exactly as she had seen them in her vision. She felt as if she was spinning, and she shook her head to clear her vision and continue painting. Moments later she was finished, and stepped back to look.

The painting began to breathe, as if actual air were passing through her lungs for the first time. A tear fell from Jacqueline's eye as she stood there, and her heart was filled with joy. Whatever the reason, Mary had come to life through her, and she gave thanks for having been the instrument through which this holy life did pass.

Diana, who had originally commissioned the painting, invited the group that had toured Medjugorje together to a private lunch attended by Father Jozo. When the painting was finally unveiled, tears began to form in his eyes. He said that the painting showed him the vast horizon that transcended religion itself, capturing the essence of universal love. What an amazing breakthrough, Jacqueline thought to herself. The painting had begun working its magic.

The next day Father Jozo began a fifteen city tour with the painting and he asked to keep it in his room that first night. He could feel the Mother's presence all around him and couldn't sleep at all. The next morning, the group gathered around a table and Father Jozo described how the painting had taken him to a new level. Then Jacqueline showed him the miraculous candle. "Yes, she is here," he said to them. "She is the Mother of All. And she is asking us to wake up to God... to live our lives with love and unity."

The tour began later that day and masses of people came to see the new painting. The gallery was filled with people who had come to view what they had heard was a most extraordinary work of art. Only a handful knew of the miracles that had accompanied the painting. Most in attendance had some association with either Medjugorje or the renewal center, but no one could possibly have anticipated the experience that was to follow.

A strange thing seemed to happen to each person who approached the painting, which was set on a tripod against the far wall. When they entered the gallery everyone was lively and alert, talkative, but as they walked toward the painting, something very unusual took place. Various conversations, which began at a normal tone near the door, slowly became quieter and quieter until the moment the visitors stood in front of Our Lady. Then there was complete silence. A small semi-circle formed around the painting — more like a vigil than an art exhibit. A feeling of solitude floated through the air, and it was strongest at point zero, directly in front of the image.

Several people seemed to go into deep meditation just standing there. A priest was so moved that he fell to his knees in prayer. When Jacqueline turned on the black light revealing the otherwise invisible light and angels, a sound like a long exhale rose above the group. No one said a word. They stood there with tears in their eyes, wondering what it meant. "It is incredible, Jacqueline," Father Jozo said as he touched her shoulder. "It takes only a small light for us to see the Light."

Then a small man from India stepped forward and broke the silence. He was a tenth generation healer, from a very respected Indian family. He alone knew what to do. He could see something that no one else could.

"Do you know that she is alive?" he asked Jacqueline. "She is alive, and she even has a pulse."

"What do you mean?" a woman asked.

"Let me show you."

He took the woman by the hand and stood her in front of the painting, then placed her finger on the spot where one would normally take a pulse. She felt silly, touching a painting in this way, but he reassured her, placing his own hands on her head.

"Now just concentrate on the woman in the painting. Feel her holiness, all the light that is coming from her body."

There was a long moment of silence. No one breathed.

"Oh, my," she said finally. "I can feel a pulse. There is an actual pulse coming from the painting."

One by one, people stepped forward, and the man put his hands on each one's head. Some fell to the ground weeping. Others were simply amazed. Jacqueline watched all this with absolute wonder. Mary had been true to her promise, she thought to herself. She had performed a miracle with paint and color... a message of love and unity in a painting.

Part Three

I had been on the 'circuit' for two-and-a-half years and was beginning to lose my fire. Most of my time was spent traveling from one conference or concert to another — an endless procession of lectures, interviews and performances. And though I was grateful to have the chance to travel around the world, extending the simple message I received in the mountains of Bosnia, I began to wonder if I was approaching the end of a very long journey. It had been a year and a half since I had seen Maria in Medjugorje, and I wondered if she had forgotten about me after all. She was the 'next teacher' the Emissaries spoke of, of that I was certain, but so much time had passed, and so little had changed. Maybe it was my own fault, I thought. Maybe I hadn't done what she asked, integrated her message about the compassionate nature of God. Whatever the reason, I had fallen into a strange melancholy, and I could feel myself sleepwalking through my public appearances as if they were routine.

And yet so many incredible things had happened in 1998. In February I was invited by the governments of both Iraq and Northern Ireland to sing the peace prayers during critical negotiations. In both cases a bulletin went out, primarily through the Internet, and millions of people around the world prayed for peace while I performed. I had no idea that there were so many people willing to open themselves in this way and become part of a movement for peace that was sweeping the planet. Maybe the Emissaries were right, I thought to myself. Maybe we were ready to create a world that reflected the laws of love, rather than the rules of fear.

A miracle took place three days after each vigil: In Iraq, though the war seemed inevitable, the peace accord was signed by Kofi Annan and Saddam Hussein; and in Northern Ireland the delegates from the political parties had a breakthrough in the peace talks that allowed them to sign the agreement a month ahead of schedule. It was an incredible honor to have been part of both these miraculous processes, and I found myself thinking that perhaps Maria's prophesy was at hand.

In April we took another incredible step towards realizing this New World. I had become very close friends with two well known speakers — Gregg Braden and Doreen Virtue. We met at a conference in Houston and immediately knew that we had an important job to do together. We decided to continue the momentum created by the Iraq and Northern Ireland peace vigils, and together we organized "The Great Experiment." The "Experiment" was formed around a very simple question: What would happen if millions of people focused their minds, and prayed for peace at the same moment? Could such a global event be scientifically measured, proving once and for all what the mystics have always told us, that we have the power to change the world simply by changing our thoughts about the world? I had already been invited to perform for forty ambassadors at the United Nations Church Center in New York on April 23rd. On the same day Gregg would be crossing over into Tibet with a group of people. It seemed like the perfect opportunity, and within days we put together the bulletin and began e-mailing it around the world.

There was no way we could have known how important this "Great Experiment" would become. Some estimates say that between five and ten million people in at least eighty countries participated. It was as if the whole world suddenly stopped and united in a revolution of love, a movement of prayer the likes of which the world had never seen before. The United Nations was abuzz in a way that no one expected. Though the concert for the ambassadors was a private event, hundreds of people called the UN switchboard trying to get information and gain admittance. Even though they were told not to come, large groups of people wandered outside hoping to "crash" the concert. And many of them succeeded, miraculously finding their way into the right building and the right room.

Fifteen minutes before the ambassadors arrived, the organizers of the event asked me to join them in a prayer circle. After several people expressed their joy at the event that was about to take place, a woman stepped into the center of the group and said something I could barely believe.

"Four years, four months, four weeks and four days ago, a group of Hopi elders were invited to the United Nations to give their vision of the New World. One of the things they said was that exactly four years, four months, four weeks and four days from that date something would occur in this building which would change the world forever. This is the day that was prophesied by those grandfathers. This is the beginning of a new era of peace."

When the scheduled moment finally arrived, a profound silence fell over the entire room. It felt as if millions of prayers were raining from the sky. I have never experienced such peace and grace before, and I knew the woman who stepped into the center of the circle had been absolutely right. Something had shifted; we all felt it. No one knew how it would reveal itself, but we turned a corner that day, and a New World was born.

Every day thereafter, as I looked back at those events, I was filled with extreme gratitude. It helped me focus on what was really important, on what I knew had to be done, and it took my mind away from the sudden lack of energy and commitment I was still feeling. It was still there, that strange loneliness that followed me like a shadow, but by then it was more like the quiet pulse of a drum, the rhythmic pattern one hears far in the distance, haunting and familiar.

At that point I hadn't had a home for nearly three years. The demand to speak and perform was overwhelming, and welcomed. But it dug a hole in my soul that sorely needed filling. I needed to feel the groundedness I experienced when I was in the presence of Maria. I cannot describe how she made me feel, only that it was the closest to "home" that I have ever been. Beyond her entrancing beauty, beyond even the wisdom that flowed from her so freely, there was an energy that defies description, and that is who she really was. It was this light I craved and dreamed of. It was the only drink that could satisfy my thirst.

A few months later, I made ready for an upcoming conference of light workers, eagerly anticipating the chance to see Gregg and Doreen again. It was the first time since we had met in Houston that we would be together at the same conference. It was exactly what I needed, I thought to myself. They would remind me of why I began this journey. And, although I didn't know why, I had the strong conviction that they would help me reconnect with Maria.

When people get together and focus on what is important, it sometimes shifts our energy away from the monotonous rhythm to which we have become accustomed. And though my life was filled with adventure and opportunity, I sensed that I had forgotten why I was there, why I had listened to the Emissaries in the first place.

There was one more reason to hope this conference would shake me from the melancholy I felt: Gregg, Doreen and I had organized another worldwide peace vigil called, "There's Nothing to Fear," for November 13, 1998. And though we did not know it when we set the date, the US and its allies were once again on the brink of attacking Iraq. Saddam Hussein had forced the UN inspectors out of Baghdad and refused to give in to international pressure. Negotiations were at a standstill, and war once again seemed inevitable.

Gregg, Doreen and I arrived in West Palm Beach, Florida, and began planning our response to this new crisis. Word about the vigil had spread around the world and it was obviously no accident that we were together at the same conference. I was the opening speaker at the conference and Doreen would speak later that evening.

During my talk, I spoke of the need to see peace as a *present* reality, not one we are trying to achieve. "If we focus on the conflict in Iraq and try to resolve it, then we are actually adding to the conflict," I said. "What we focus on increases. If we focus our minds on the peace that is already present, as if it has already been achieved, then our prayers energetically connect with the solution, not the conflict." I had heard this from the Emissaries themselves, and I believed it to be true. At that moment, however, the words echoed within me, looking for a solid place to land.

During Doreen's talk, Gregg and I joined her on the stage. When the moment came for the vigil to begin, we asked the audience to feel themselves united with everyone in the world praying for peace at that very moment. "This Single Mind has the power to bring peace where conflict seems to reign," Doreen said. "The decision we make for global harmony will sweep over the world, and everyone who believes that war is an option, in Iraq or anywhere else, will change their minds and join us in this revolution now and forever. This is the moment that peace has prevailed. Together we acknowledge this shift and we give thanks that we have been used as instruments of peace."

None of us knew that President Clinton had just ordered NATO to strike Iraq. Within minutes the fighter jets were in the air prepared to carry out their orders. But once again a miracle occurred that no one expected. Three hours after the vigil took place, Saddam Hussein sent a message to the UN saying he would allow the inspectors to return. President Clinton heard this news and ordered the fighter pilots to stand down. But the chess game was still not over. Once again President Clinton ordered the jets to attack, and moments before they released the bombs he ordered them down a second time. No one quite knew why. Tense hours and days passed, but the conflict was avoided, and peace had its way once more.

We were overjoyed by this development. Though none of us felt personally responsible for this miraculous turn of events, we knew that millions of people focusing their minds on peace had had a profound effect.

I remembered when Maria reminded me of the promise I had made when I was twelve years old. I had asked her to make me her instrument, to use me to bring peace to the world. I began to realize that God is always willing to use us in this way, in fact it is the one prayer that God always hears. We are all asked to give ourselves to the world, and to allow our gifts to be used to promote healing and peace. Even something as simple as a prayer can be used by God, for it adds momentum to every thought, every aspiration expressed by every person on earth. When we surrender to the Divine pulse within us, then we act as one mind, one heart beating for a transformed world. This is what I learned from these prayer vigils.

After Doreen finished her talk, I was standing near the front of the room chatting with several people when I felt someone's hand on my shoulder. I turned around and saw a woman with deep, penetrating eyes standing next to me, and I immediately gave her my full attention.

"My name is Jacqueline Ripstein," she said. "I am an artist and have several of my paintings on display at this conference. There is one in particular that I want you to see."

She took me by the hand and led me over to the side of the room where three paintings stood on tripods. We stopped in front of one of them — a beautiful painting of Mary floating on a cloud. I was immediately entranced.

"This is called *Our Lady of the Universe*," she said. "I have read your book, *Emissary of Light*, and I know that you have been to Medjugorje. This painting was commissioned by a renewal center for children just outside the village. But it appears to have also been commissioned by someone else. Miracles seem to happen every time the painting is displayed. It has a special power, as if it has been blessed by Our Lady."

I did not make the connection between this painting and my experience with Maria right away. I looked at it for a moment and commended her on her talent, then started to excuse myself. I was tired from the eventful evening and needed to rest. Jacqueline said that she would like to have a talk with me before the conference was over, and I said we would try. In all honesty I didn't believe I would have the time, and since I did not feel compelled, at least not at that moment, I had no desire to make the time. The energy I felt after the vigil was so strong that I didn't want to make commitments to anyone.

That night I fell into a deep sleep and had a series of amazing dreams. In one I was back in Bosnia with the Emissaries, sitting with Teacher, the leader of the community. He sat there looking across the fire at me, but didn't say a word. It was very unusual because this was the very place where we had most of our talks. I watched the sparks as they flew between and above us and waited for him to speak. He never did.

Next I found myself in Jerusalem where I had been several months earlier. I was walking around the chapel that now stands where Mary is said to have lived two thousand years ago, a round room with beautiful paintings lining the wall. But the paintings were not the same as those I had seen during my actual visit. As I stopped and looked at each one I realized that they were scenes from my own life. The first was me as a child making my promise to Mary. In the second I was in the monastery praying in front of her statue. Next I saw myself in the mountains of Bosnia sitting at the fire with Teacher, then in Medjugorje sitting next to the peace pole with Maria.

There was one last painting, and it was the only one that left me confused. It was Jacqueline's painting, *Our Lady of the Universe*. I was suddenly struck by how similar she looked to the version of Maria I had met on the hill. The structure of the face was almost identical. And yet I wondered why every other painting reflected events that had already occurred in my life, all but the last. I had the feeling it represented something that was *going* to happen.

In the final dream I was in Iraq, sitting in the lobby of the El Rasheed Hotel. This was where I had spent most of my time while I was in Baghdad, watching the hundreds of reporters as they carried equipment in and out of the hotel, or patiently waiting for Mr. Sabar, my guide. As I sat watching the scene, I suddenly felt someone sit down on the couch next to me. I turned and saw Teacher, the old Emissary who in my previous dream hadn't said a word.

"Are you getting the picture yet?" he asked.

"Is that supposed to be a joke or something? I take it you're referring to the painting that woman showed me."

"If you think this is about a painting, you're in trouble," he said. "With everything that has happened to you, I hoped you would be a bit quicker. The painting is a symbol of who she is, just like the woman you saw in Medjugorje was a symbol. In other words, it has nothing to do with what it looks like. The truth is beneath... under the surface. She could have appeared to you any way she wanted. She chose a way that would teach you a lesson. And now you have seen her again, but because you're stuck on the image, you missed it completely."

"What do you mean? Are you still talking about the painting?"

"I'm talking about her plan, which you still don't know about, but which is about to begin. Everything has led to this — your experience with the Emissaries, the prayer vigils, meeting Maria on the hill. And just as you've sensed every time millions of people have gathered together in prayer, the shift is about to occur. Everything you've ever learned is about to be put to the test."

"What exactly is the shift?" I asked him.

"She told you what it is. Humanity is about to step into the energy you call compassion. It's the feminine nature of God that Maria spoke of. But there's more to it than that. One of the byproducts of that shift is that people will learn to access this energy directly. You've relied on other people's experiences for too long. Miracles or apparitions occur in places like Medjugorje and everyone flocks to hear what was said. But they don't believe that they can be part of the experience. It is easier to let someone else talk to God while you ask them questions later.

"And that's what's about to change," he continued. "It's time for people to experience this energy for themselves. That's how humanity will take the next step, the step through the Door. You need to have a direct experience of the Love of God, and that's her main role — to help people do that. Since she is the embodiment of compassion, or the feminine energy of the Divine, she is the one who will move people's hearts and open them to real peace."

"I've been waiting for something to happen for a long time now," I said. "When I saw the comet a year and a half ago, I thought that everything was going to speed up. Instead it seems to have slowed down."

"Sometimes the fruit needs to wait on the vine a bit longer than it thinks before it is ripe," Teacher said. "Everything has been happening in perfect order, and you have done everything you can. You just don't think you have, but that's going to change. That's why I'm here with you now, to make sure you're paying attention."

"What about the painting?" I asked. "I know there's something important about it or it wouldn't have shown up in my dream."

"As I said — pay attention. You are in the right place... that's all I can tell you. You will soon have all the information you need to take the next step. And to answer a question you didn't really ask. Don't worry, she hasn't forgotten you."

That was all I could remember the next morning. I immediately sat down at my desk and wrote down the entire dream, in as much detail as I could recall. I was not going to miss a thing, I thought to myself. If this was where the adventure would finally come together, then I wanted to make sure I was prepared.

The next morning I set out to find Jacqueline. Hundreds of people filled the hallway that led to the conference room, and I wasn't sure I would have time to find her before the morning session. As I passed the dining room, I heard someone call my name.

"James... please come and sit with us." Jacqueline was with several friends eating breakfast and they quickly made room for me. I sat down, poured a cup of coffee and took a deep breath.

"I'm glad you saw me," I said nervously. "I was in fact looking for you, but with all these people... "

"We have something we would like to ask you." It was Connie who spoke this time, a beautiful Hispanic woman who had been with Jacqueline the previous day. "We believe that there is power in the combination of different art forms. It has been our mission to share Jacqueline's painting with as many people as possible, but we believe it will touch even more people if it is accompanied by music."

"We would like you to write one or two songs that could accompany the painting," Jacqueline said, continuing her thought. "I have had this idea ever since I read your book, and especially when we heard you sing last night. There is a quality in your music that resonates with this painting, and I believe it will add to its power. I know that we have just met and that this request is rather sudden, but I would be honored if you would consider it."

"It's not as unexpected as you might believe," I said. "Please tell me more about the painting... about the energy you said it seems to have."

"Oh, that is a very long story," Jacqueline said. "First of all, I am not Catholic, in fact I am not even a Christian, but Jewish. And yet, as an artist I do not cling to any one religion, but to all religion. It was still strange when I was commissioned to paint *Our Lady of the Universe*. I didn't know if I was the right person to paint it. I thought, surely there was an artist with a more personal connection with Our Lady. I decided that I would need to receive a sign if I were to accept. The pencil sketches I had been experimenting with helped me feel more comfortable, for I felt a strong energy coming from them, even at that early stage. But I needed more, and I prayed to Our Lady to show me her will.

Jacqueline went on to describe the entire incident with the vigil candle, how the image had appeared on the glass, matching in every detail the sketch she had already made.

"Tell him about the letters," Connie said.

"Oh, yes, there were some strange looking wax impressions above the painting, and I realized they were Hebrew letters. Unfortunately I cannot read Hebrew so I invited a rabbi into my home to have a look. He told me they were not just random letters. They were whole words, and they read, 'God exists, and makes miracles.' Well you can imagine how I felt. All I can say is that I didn't waste any time after that."

"When she finished the painting, several showings were immediately arranged," Connie said. "That was when we realized that it was truly from Heaven. People went into altered states just looking at it. It had an energy that touched people very deeply, and we knew that Our Lady had a special plan for it."

I was overjoyed and afraid all at the same time. It was beginning to come together, everything I had learned from Teacher and my discussion with Maria. They had both spoken about the need for people to experience the Divine directly, not through others. And that's what seemed to be happening with this painting. The only question left was, how did I fit in?

"I don't know the answer to that question," Jacqueline said, shaking her head. "But I feel you are involved somehow. Once again, there is something about your music that resonates with the painting. It's as if they go together in some way."

Later that day I found a few moments to be alone with the painting. As I stood there in front of it I began to feel a somewhat familiar sensation. It was the same feeling I had had when I was with Maria in Medjugorje, though to a lesser degree. But it was there nonetheless. For the first time since we had been together on the hill I knew she was calling me. I could feel her presence again, and it filled me with an amazing energy.

"What do you feel?" a voice behind me asked. I turned around and saw Jacqueline standing behind me. "Do you sense anything unusual?"

"What do you think it means?" I asked, purposefully avoiding her question. "It has to have a purpose, some higher reason or calling. What do you think it is?"

"I believe that many blessings are coming to the world right now," she said, "as if we have entered a very special period in history. I also believe that Our Lady has a special role to play, at least the energy she extends and represents."

"And what is that?"

"She represents love... peace. That's why she is called the Queen of Peace. I believe that this is the time humanity will enter into her energy, the energy of compassion. People will begin to want that experience more than anything else, and she will be there to give it to them."

"But you're Jewish," I said, nudging her a bit to see where she would go. "Are you telling me that she will play the same role for everyone, regardless of their religion or faith?"

"First of all, Mary was Jewish as well," she said. "And I also don't believe this has anything to do with religion, but with the love that transcends religion. Our Lady's role is not to convert everyone to Catholicism, but to bring them into the grace of God that knows no boundaries. She may appear in one form to one person, and look completely different to the next. But it is still her... whoever she is. It is still the grace of God that is being showered down on the whole world. That is what she represents."

"How do you think this painting will bring people to that experience?"

"I have no idea," she said. "It really is none of my business, but hers. Here, I want to show you something."

Jacqueline walked over to the painting and turned on a black light that was attached to the top. Suddenly beams of light appeared above Maria and covered her in a magical glow.

"This is called Invisible Art and Light technique," she said as she stepped back from the painting. "It is something I invented. In normal light it appears one way, and when you turn on the black lamp, the beams of light emerge. It is also a brilliant metaphor. If we look with our physical eyes we see only the surface of the message. But when we look with our spiritual eyes we see so much more. We see the light that is given as a gift from Heaven. And isn't it interesting that a black light is used to see the whole picture? In the same way we must go into our own darkness, the things that we hide from others because we are ashamed, in order to unleash the light within. It is only when we give our whole selves to God, the good and the bad, the positive and the negative, that we are enlightened."

I was amazed at her sensitivity and insight. We were the same in so many ways, especially in that single desire to be used as instruments of peace. She did it with a brush, and I did it with sound. What would happen if we combined these two media? Perhaps this is what Maria had in mind all along, to bring all of her children together and initiate the shift so many different people were talking about. I wondered if I should tell my story to Jacqueline, the story of Maria and how she changed my life. For some reason I decided not to, but to wait a bit longer. Something was about to happen, something that would bring all the loose pieces together. I would wait until I had more perspective, until I felt the ground beneath my feet again.

"What do you want me to do?" I asked her.

"I don't think I have the right to ask you to do anything," she said as she touched my arm. "This is not my project. I'm just like you — following orders. You need to ask her that question."

"I have already," I said, "and I think I have an answer. Let me spend some time with the painting and see what music comes. If this is what she really wants, then it will be effortless. I agree with everything you've said, Jacqueline. Combining these two art forms would be very powerful. It would amplify the experiences people are already having. I believe that music and art have the special quality of sliding past the intellect and going straight to the heart. That's why their effects are not rational, at least not from a mental point of view. But from the spirit's point of view it is completely rational, and that's why we instinctively gravitate to the arts."

"Then it is up to her," she said. "We will be her instruments and let her use us in any way she wants. And if this painting and your music are part of her plan... then so it is."

I felt a bond with Jacqueline that I cannot explain, as if we had made an ancient pact that was finally being realized. I spent the rest of the conference waiting — I'm not sure for what. But I knew *something* was going to happen. We had come to a critical point in our journey, and I knew the waiting was over. I would not act on my own, but wait for Maria to tell me what to do. And I knew she would.

Two days later, I was on a jet flying from Denver to San Francisco. Jacqueline had given me a business card size photo of the painting, and I had meditated with it for hours. It made me feel close to Maria again — flooding me with the feeling of love I had felt on the hill in Medjugorje a year and a half earlier. It was almost as if the picture vibrated with her presence, filling me with an overwhelming sense of gratitude. "What do you want me to do?" I asked her. "You've brought me so far, and I know we're near the end. Please don't make me wait any longer. I'll do anything for you, but you have to tell me what that is."

Suddenly something happened which I cannot fully explain. I felt myself in many places at once, as if my spirit had suddenly jumped dimensions and I was fully aware of many levels of reality. Though I still perceived my body on the jet, deep in meditation, I was also aware of myself in several other places. The ribbons of time had converged and linear movement ceased to exist. Though it would be impossible to fully explain the sensation, I can narrow it down to three separate experiences. First there was the physical sensation of sitting on the jet. Second, I felt as if I was with Teacher again, sitting at the fire in the mountains of Bosnia. And finally, I was on the hill with Maria, exactly the same as I had been before. Each one of these experiences was whole and complete, as if they were all occurring at once. And yet I had the ability to be fully present in each one. I was fully engaged by each experience, and yet all three occurred at once.

"Do you see what is happening?" Maria asked.

"I feel what is happening, but I don't understand it. We've come to the crossroads, haven't we?"

"We've always been at the crossroads," Teacher said. "It's just that you've finally realized it."

"I'm not sure I understand."

"You have always existed in many places at the same time," Maria said. "The Door of Eternity has always been inside you. You exist on both sides of the Door. Now you're ready to experience both realities simultaneously."

"Is this what your message is really about? If I'm ready for this, then everyone's ready for it. Is that it?"

"It would be more accurate to say that you're ready to be ready," Teacher explained. "When you release your fear about what it means to be fully present to the Divine, then that which is most essential within you steps forward. It has always been there, but it has been clouded by your resistance."

"An era of peace is at hand," Maria said, "simply because humanity has begun to accept it. Every reality occurs together, and every possible reality. The world of fear sits beside the world of love, and you always choose the world you want to perceive. The revolution of love is the choice to see past the shadow of reality to reality itself. That is the real meaning of the Door of Eternity. It is a metaphor, just like everything else."

"So the Door of Eternity reflects the choice between love and fear," I said. "When we choose love, the world changes as well."

"The world you perceive is the result of that single decision," Teacher said to me. "It is like turning on a light. The room that was dark a moment ago is suddenly illuminated. You are able to see things that were once invisible to your sight. They were always there. The only thing that changes is your willingness to see them."

"And that is why you are here…" Maria went on, "at the crossroads, as you put it. And humanity itself is here with you. You cannot make a decision that does not involve everyone. This is the time of transformation, and this transformation will occur when people enter the Door themselves. They will do this by coming into direct contact with the Divine. You can no longer rely upon anyone else's testimony, but upon your own experience. God is there for everyone, and the experience of the Divine is always waiting. All that is needed is the willingness to enter. The rest is the gift of God."

"You and Jacqueline have been given a very important gift," Teacher said. "Her painting and your music will be a bridge for many people, an access point for them to enter into this experience."

"I want you to go to a recording studio in three days," she said. "I will be there with you, and I will enter into your music. You will sing to me, and I will sing back to the world. Sound and art possess a special quality that is unparalleled. Spiritual energy can be attached to both, imprinted upon the sound and light waves. The ego does not understand this process, and therefore cannot interfere with it. It slides past the mind altogether and touches the spirit. When you sing your songs, I will imprint my energy onto the sound waves. I have already done this with the painting. When combined, when the music and the painting are experienced together, many people will be healed, and thousands will come into direct contact with their Divine nature."

"Don't worry about what you will sing," Teacher said. "Everything will be given to you. You have asked to be made into an instrument of peace. Well, here you are. Step back into the Divine and let yourself be used. Give your voice to God and let Divine Light flow from the song you sing. This is what you've been waiting for. The gift of the Spirit is at hand."

I cannot find the words that would begin to explain what happened next. Waves of love flowed over me, filling me with compassion for all beings, revealing every mystery of the universe. I suddenly saw the whole picture, as if reality itself suddenly opened before me. A curtain was raised on a New World. I felt Maria and Teacher as I never had before, as if they were not outside or separate from me at all. Light and darkness flowed together as well, as if they were different aspects of one reality. I passed into a different realm, and yet I didn't move at all. Everything changed, and nothing changed. There are no words to describe what happened to me while I sat there on that flight to San Francisco, but the world has not looked the same since.

It was as if I woke up from a dream. The captain's voice came through the speakers asking the flight attendants to prepare for landing. I struggled to move, desperately trying to hold onto what had just happened to me. The seat belt was at my side and I was finally able to pull it over my lap and fasten it together. Long moments passed as the jet descended. I felt myself descend as well, as if I was falling from Heaven. I could feel my body again, but now the sensation of being physical was strange to me. Something was different, but I wasn't sure what it was. The experience with Teacher and Maria was more real than anything I had ever known. And yet there was no context in which it could be related, to myself or to others.

When we finally landed, I found myself filled with a strange sensation. Fear and exaltation stood side by side, and I wondered which one was appropriate. As I left the jet, I could still feel Teacher's and Maria's presence. And yet, I hadn't had time to integrate what had just occurred. I felt like a baby suddenly pushed from its mother's womb. I was in a New World, and I didn't have any idea how to relate to it.

I am in the habit of turning on my cell phone the instant I leave a flight and when I did, I saw that I had one message. I pushed the button to see who had called.

"Jimmy, it's Shrinat Devi. I need to talk to you right away. Please call me as soon as possible."

I couldn't believe my ears. It had been well over a year since I spoke with her last, the woman who told me I had to meet Maria in Medjugorje. How could she have known to call me at that precise moment? I dialed the number without hesitating and my pulse began to race. Something else was happening that I couldn't explain. The fact that my experience on the jet was of a subjective nature made it harder for me to accept. Meeting

Maria in Medjugorje was completely different since it was physical and direct. The fact that Shrinat Devi had tried to call me, perhaps at the same moment I was having my experience, offered possible support for its credibility.

"Jimmy, I'm so glad you called," she said as soon as she answered. "Where are you right now?"

"I just got off a plane in San Francisco," I said. "Before you say another word, I need to know why you called when you did. What is happening?"

"An hour ago I was meditating and I felt the presence of the Blessed Mother," she said as her voice suddenly became quiet and respectful. "She told me to call and ask you a question. She wants to know if you're listening to her call. There's something she said to you and she wants to know if you heard her."

I was stunned and I couldn't speak for a long moment. My experience with Maria and Teacher had begun approximately one hour earlier. It was almost as if Maria finished with me, then got on the phone and called Shrinat Devi to make sure I had been listening. It was just the proof I was looking for.

"Yes I am listening," I said. "What else did she say?"

"Only that she loves you very much. I don't know what she said to you, but from the feeling I had, it must be very important."

I took the Santa Rosa shuttle to the San Rafael depot where my friend Bea was waiting. The entire trip was a blur of awe and gratitude. Maria was keeping her promise, I thought. Just when I felt everything was about to end, it had jumped to a whole new level of excitement.

Bea and I walked to a Thai restaurant in downtown San Rafael and sat down to eat. I tried to tell her about the last few days, ever since I'd been to the conference in Florida and met Jacqueline, but my mind was still too unsettled to think straight. And how could I explain it? I had no way of relating the experience I'd had during the flight, and the rest was still a vague series of fantastic happenings.

Halfway through the meal the cell phone began to ring.

"Hello Jimmy, it's Maria Christina from Argentina."

There are three women in my life who anchor my 'Mary Connection'. The first is Shrinat Devi who had told me to go back to Medjugorje because Mary had a message for me. The second is a friend named Danielle. And finally there is Maria Christina Urhart, from Buenos Aires, Argentina, who, more than any woman I have ever known, holds what I call the 'Mary Energy'. Whenever I'm with her I feel as if I'm back on the hill in Medjugorje, sitting once again with her namesake. I had not talked to Maria Christina for several months, so the suddenness of her call shocked me.

"About two hours ago I was meditating and I felt the Blessed Mother's presence," she said. "She told me to ask you if you're listening to her message."

I was well past overwhelmed, and Maria Christina's call nearly pushed me over the edge. Only one more call was required, I thought. These things happen in threes — that's how you know you're in the presence of a miracle... at least that's what I've always believed. Shrinat Devi and Maria Christina had the same message, and I knew there was still one more waiting. An hour later I was in the car with Bea and the phone rang again.

"Jimmy, how are you? It's Danielle."

"Don't tell me," I said, "You have a message for me from Our Lady."

"How could you have known that?"

"It's a very long but amazing story," I said. "But I don't want to interrupt you. Tell me everything."

"Several hours ago I was praying and felt Mary's presence. I could actually hear her, just like I'm hearing you now. She said the same thing three times, and by the third I realized that she wanted me to write it down. So I did. I want to read it now because it's a message for you."

I asked Bea to pull the car over so I could give Danielle my full attention. "Okay, I'm ready," I told her.

"This is what Maria asked me to tell you:

> *"Open your heart, my dear One, and listen to the sound of my voice as it echoes in the depth of your heart. I am your Mother, and I am here to lead you into the Light. Reach out your hand to these others, the ones who have claimed this same reward, and walk together into the arms of the Divine. This is the time you have been waiting for, the time of the great awakening. You have been with me since the very beginning, and you are with me now. Let my Community reemerge, fulfilling the promise*

and mission you have held since the beginning of time. Are you listening to me, Beloved? Open to the sound of my voice, and I will lead you home.
        Your Mother.[1]

Danielle paused and said quietly, "That's it, the entire message."

"What do you think it means?" I asked her, trying to hide how much the message meant to me.

"I feel that something is about to happen, something of global significance. And we're all part of it. She said this is a time of great awakening. That can be confusing unless you understand who she really is. Mary is the embodiment of the compassion of God. Therefore, an era of compassion is at hand. Mary is the bearer of that message because compassion is normally seen as a feminine quality, as opposed to the masculine qualities of power and redemption which were anchored by Jesus."

"Are you saying that we're entering a new age?" I asked.

"I don't like those words, 'New Age,' because they're loaded. They don't really mean anything anymore. Fifteen years ago it described a movement toward the esoteric traditions of all religions. Therefore, there was nothing 'new' about it. Then people from traditional churches became very afraid because they felt it was leading people into confusion. And in some ways they were right. The essence of the spiritual traditions to which people found themselves drawn was being watered down, and all that was left were candy coated versions of the original wisdom.

"But to answer your question, yes, this is a new age we're entering. But it is not about crystals and channeling. The era that Mary is proclaiming is about channeling the Light of God. Each one of us is called to be a channel of peace, and that's the essence of her message. It's not some weird thing that turns people off, but the real focus of every spiritual path."

I thanked Danielle for her words of wisdom and tucked the phone away.

There was one final thing that had to happen before Maria's message to me was complete. She said that in three days I would go into a studio and record music to accompany the painting. Since I hadn't planned to record anything like this while I was in San Francisco, I wondered how it would happen. Then I remembered a friend who managed a recording

1. This message has been altered from the original.

studio located in a church at the Presidio, the former military base that now housed hundreds of nonprofit organizations. A year earlier Colin and I had worked on a project together, and it seemed the perfect fit. I set out to arrange an impromptu concert to be held in the church, to be recorded just as Maria had instructed.

Several friends were invited to attend this very special event. What was going to happen? Maria said that she would enter the music, actually imprint herself onto the sound waves. The possibilities of such a miracle astounded me. She spoke of the need for people to come into the direct experience of the Divine, and that something would be activated within them when they looked at the painting and listened to the music at the same time. There was no way for me to understand what this meant, but there was also no reason for me to doubt it. I was past the point of doubt, considering everything that had already happened. The atmosphere was charged with a feeling of trust, and I was ready to play my part in this unusual drama.

The microphones were set into place and the audience was ready. I took the small photograph of the painting that Jacqueline had given me, and placed it in the wire mesh of the large studio mike. As soon as Colin gave me the word I took a deep breath and began to play. I sang the Hail Mary, a version I had written a year earlier, then several other songs I had written several days before. The energy seemed to be building, and I wondered how Maria was going to keep her promise, to enter into the music and imprint her energy onto the sound waves.

I thought I had sung the last song. The strings of the guitar were still vibrating and the sound of my voice echoed in the back of the church. That was when I felt her, just as I had felt her on the hill in Medjugorje, and on the flight to San Francisco. I knew she was there, but I couldn't tell how, or where.

I looked down at the picture that I had stuck between the wires of the microphone. It was different somehow, as if it moved in front of my eyes. I felt a bit dizzy and my vision started to blur for a moment — the same feeling Jacqueline had when she tried to paint Our Lady's eyes. Time seemed to stop and I closed my eyes, wondering what was happening. When I opened them again I looked at the picture. Her face was different. A moment earlier she was looking down and to the right. Now she was looking straight at me, her eyes live and real. They blinked, and somehow I wasn't surprised, almost as if I expected it to happen. For a long moment we looked at each other. And that was when the picture seemed to speak.

I wasn't sure if I heard her with my ears or with my mind. They seemed the same at that moment. But I will never forget what she said, words that came from an image on a picture no bigger than a business card. I felt like I was twelve years old again, when I first heard the voice. It filled me, just as it had then.

"Sing what I say to you," she whispered. "I will give you the words, and you will give me the music." Without thinking, I began to sing the words I heard:

"The light is in you, open the Door, feel me as I enter.

Your heart is mine, I will claim you, Divine One,

Know me as I enter inside you now.

For I am your mother, I will give you all that you need

to spread the light of Divinity all around."

The words and the music kept coming, I'm not sure how long for. I had entered into a deep trance and the music flowed without effort or thought. My eyes were fixed on the picture of Maria, the beautiful image that Jacqueline had painted, and the entire world seemed to stand still.

Then it ended as abruptly as it had begun. The picture had returned to its original position and everything seemed normal again. There was a strange energy pulsing through my body and I jumped up from the chair and began pacing back and forth. My friends looked at me and wondered what had happened. They felt something, but they didn't know what it was. I told them about my experience, the way she came to life and spoke to me. She had entered the music, and we all knew it. In that moment everything came together, the painting, the music, the energy. What would happen now, I wondered? It had never been up to me, and it still wasn't.

I closed my eyes and saw her in my mind's eye. "Thank you, my Beloved," I said to her. "Thank you for not forgetting me."

Part Four

he world around us is changing. This is obvious at the physical level where we see the exponential growth in technology and the changes in populations and political systems. And if we focus our awareness on the more subtle levels of feelings and emotions, we see changes there also. Maria helps us open to love and compassion, but it is up to us to take the next step, to open the Door into the direct experience of the Love of God. Though aided by all the Powers of Heaven, this is still our responsibility, as was made vividly clear when I went with a companion to the refugee camps in Macedonia.

"I hate to be the one to tell you this, but you're not going to be able to get into any of the Kosovo refugee camps," the man said.

The bus that Gillian and I were on had just crossed the border of Macedonia from Bulgaria, and at about the same time we realized we were sitting next to an American journalist who was also on his way to Skopje. His speech was slow and deliberate, and he seemed irritated at the idea of us going into the camps to perform a peace concert and focus a world-wide prayer vigil.

"Why do you think it's impossible?" Gillian asked him.

"I have been in and out of the camps ever since this conflict began," he said as he leaned over toward us, making sure we wouldn't miss a single word. "There are police checks all along the way. The only way to get past them is to have press credentials from both the Macedonian government and NATO itself. In order to get those credentials you have to have a press pass issued by a legitimate press service. You don't have that... you just want to go in and, as far as they know, get in the way of the people who really are helping."

I could feel Gillian getting angry at the man, so I leaned between them and asked, "How can we get credentials?" The incredulous look on his face deepened.

"You're not listening, are you?" he said. "You can't get them... you don't have a press pass. It's the only way, unless you're smuggled in on a Red Cross truck or something. You clearly have no idea how difficult things are there. NATO has gotten most of the refugees out of the open fields and into tents, but there are hundreds of thousands of them who still have nothing. They're starving to death and have no shelter. You may as well turn around, because you have no way of helping them."

Two hours later the bus pulled into the bus station at Skopje, and our journalist friend offered us luck as he got into a cab. "I don't believe that man," Gillian said to me as we watched him leave. "He has no idea what he's talking about."

"He may know what he's talking about, but he doesn't understand what we're really here for. I don't care how difficult it is, if we're supposed to make it into the camps then we will. By the way, I haven't told you about the dream I had last night, have I?"

"What dream?"

"Last night I kept seeing a small woman in a white nun's habit darting in and out of doors and through alleys. She never said anything but at one point, when she looked straight at me, I realized who it was. It was Mother Teresa. That's why I'm wearing this shirt."

I unbuttoned and removed my outer shirt to reveal the T-shirt I was wearing. There was a picture of Mother Teresa on my chest, with a radiant smile that illumined magical eyes. The pupil of one of the eyes was shaped like a dove, as if it was reflecting in her iris.

"That's beautiful," Gillian said. "But do you think it's a good idea to wear it here in Macedonia? She was an ethnic Albanian, you know, and Albanians are not very popular here, especially now."

"But she was also born here in Skopje," I said. "That makes it a very good idea. I have a feeling she was telling me something in my dream last night, like she's paving the way for us. Besides, how can anyone say 'no' to us with her staring them in the eyes?"

"Well, how do you suggest we begin? I'm inclined to believe that the journalist was right about NATO. They probably won't want to help us."

"But what if they do?" I said to her. "It's definitely the most direct path. If they say 'no' then we can try other routes."

It was three in the afternoon, only three hours before the prayer vigil would begin, not much time to get the necessary credentials and then find the nearest camp. Meeting the journalist was in some ways a blessing. It was his warning that showed us how limited our options were. He also told us where to begin — at NATO headquarters located at the Hotel Continental. Without hesitation we stopped a cab and were on our way there.

When we arrived at NATO headquarters we found the appropriate office and rang the small bell on the desk. Seconds later a French officer stepped out of the back and sat down in front of us.

"May I help you?" he asked dryly.

"I hope so," I said. "I was told that this is where we need to go to get our credentials to get into the nearest refugee camp."

"Press pass, please," he said, just as he had probably done hundreds of times before.

"Well, that's where we have a problem," I said to him. "We're not really from the press, though I am an author, if that makes a difference."

"Why do you want to get to the camp then?" He set his pen down on the desk and gave us his full attention. This was clearly out of the ordinary, and he seemed ready to respond.

"We're here representing millions of people around the world who will be saying prayers of peace for these people at 6 p.m. local time. We've done this in the past in places like Iraq, Northern Ireland and Israel, and we've always found that it was important to have someone at ground zero, someone who can anchor the prayers."

I wondered if I had said too much. It might have been better to stick to the "I'm an author working on a book" slant. Instead I had veered into esoteric 'la la' land, and it felt like quicksand. The soldier sat looking into my eyes, and I was sure we were done.

"Okay, is this for both of you?" he asked as he picked his pen up again and began writing on a sheet of paper.

"Yes," Gillian said to him.

"My suggestion is that you say you're free lance reporters. Hopefully the Ministry of Information won't want to see your press pass... maybe they'll assume I checked it already."

"That's where we have to go next?" I asked.

"Yes. Any cab driver will know where it is. And by the way, I'm glad you're doing whatever it is you said you're doing. I don't quite understand it, but I'm all for whatever works. Prayer is great."

I looked over at Gillian and smiled. The direct path had worked, amazingly enough. Minutes later we were in a cab on our way to the Ministry of Information. We were one step away. If we made it over this next hurdle, then we would have accomplished the impossible. We would then have access to the camp and would be in place to focus the prayer vigil.

The Ministry of Information looked like an ordinary office building, and it surprised me that the long line of journalists I had been told to expect was nowhere to be seen. It had seemed that would be the final obstacle. I had heard that it sometimes took up to two days for press requests to be processed. We got out of the cab and walked to the entrance. When we opened the office door, we saw a man sitting behind a desk busily working on his computer.

"Hello, is this where we get press credentials?" I asked.

"Yes," he said without looking up. "Please sit down and wait a moment."

We sat down on the two chairs against the wall and tried to look official. Freelance reporters, I kept thinking. That's why we're here, nothing too unusual or strange, nothing to be alarmed about. Just give us whatever papers we need and we'll go report on things. We're no different than the hundreds of other journalists who have walked through this door.

"Give me your NATO credentials," he finally said, breaking my thought. Gillian and I handed him the papers and we sat back down again. He never even looked up at us, just kept his eyes on the screen and held out his hand. He looked down at the sheets we gave him and seemed to be copying information onto the computer. We watched him without moving. If he didn't ask us for our press passes, then we would be in. Just don't do anything out of the ordinary, I thought, nothing any other reporter wouldn't do.

Suddenly he stood up from his desk and began furiously grabbing stamps and folders and other things I did not see. At one point he looked over at us for a second or two, then turned away. What was he thinking, I wondered. Was he actually going for it? I glanced over at Gillian and gave her a look of confidence. We're almost there, I said to her silently. I sat back in my chair and folded one leg over the other, no reason to be concerned.

The man held out two sheets of paper and sat back down at his desk.

"Thank you," he said, then returned to his typing. We stood up and took the papers from him.

"Thank you," we said back to him, then walked out of the room. When we were outside we hugged each other in triumph.

"Looks like we're on our way," Gillian said, "and we still have two hours before the vigil begins."

As we stood at the front door three taxis pulled up and about a dozen journalists got out. They were there for the credentials we had just received, and luckily enough, we had gotten there before they did. If we had been behind them we would have never made it to the camp in time.

Gillian and I got into one of the cabs and asked the driver where the nearest refugee camp was. One never thinks of asking a question such as this; it is well outside the realm of normal possibility. And yet in this place, under these circumstances, it was the only question we could ask. I had been told that NATO had spent a great deal of time and energy setting up several camps on the outskirts of Skopje, as the solution to their most immediate problem — providing for the most basic human needs of the refugees. The driver understood immediately and we were soon off to Brazde, one of two camps just outside the city limit.

We could see the camp from at least a mile away, the immense fence that enclosed the prison-like home of some thirty-five thousand people. We had passed several police checks without incident, and when we turned down the dirt road that led to the camp I felt my stomach slowly sink. I could see hundreds of people pushed up against the fence, looking out at us — desperate faces huddled together with empty eyes and little hope. They looked at the scene beyond the fence as if it was the only world that really existed, and it was just beyond their reach. They could touch the air with their fingers and breathe the dust that rose from the wheels of the taxis and the NATO vehicles that passed them, and that was all. It was as close to freedom as they could get.

We got out of the taxi and I swung the guitar onto my back. How was I going to look, walking through the gate with nothing but a guitar, and of course, the very large bag of chocolate bars I had brought from a grocery store near Findhorn? I began to feel self-conscious about our plan. Would they have any interest at all in the prayer vigil or the peace songs I was going to sing? Most of these people were so focused on their own survival that it seemed a bit trite to approach them in this way. I felt embarrassed for a moment, and I wondered if I should abandon my plan to sing while millions of people around the world were praying.

"Trust me," I heard a voice say. "I haven't brought you this far for nothing. I am here, and everything is in order."

It was Maria, and she seemed to be speaking from within me, as if she had entered my soul. I suddenly felt her presence, her influence, and I took a long, deep breath. It soothed me in a way that is impossible to describe. Just to know that she was with me, to know that she was somehow present in all this madness, filled me with strength and renewed my energy.

"What do you want me to do," I said out loud.

"Do what you came to do. As I've said before, allow yourself to be my instrument, and I will do the work through you."

"What did you say?" It was Gillian. I had obviously spoken a bit louder than I thought. I didn't know if I should say anything to her, not that she wouldn't understand, but the situation we were in was already so incredible. To choose that moment to tell her that Maria was there would just complicate things.

"Oh, nothing," I said. "I was just talking to myself."

We walked to the gate and showed our credentials to the Macedonian soldiers there. They checked them thoroughly, then let us pass. It took me a few seconds to realize that we had actually made it. Everyone had said it was impossible, that we would never be able to make it this far. And yet there we were, standing on the inside of the fence that separated the refugees from the world. It couldn't have been smoother, and I reached to my chest and touched the picture of Mother Teresa on my shirt.

Thanks for paving the way for us, I said to her. I know you're probably here somewhere, doing what you can.

As soon as we entered the camp, people began walking up to us from every direction to ask a single question, "Telephone?" Their physical needs had been met, though just barely, and they were away from the dangerous Serbian army. Now all they wanted was to make a phone call, to let their relatives know they were still alive. We felt helpless already, unable to give them what they needed. I knew I had to trust, to focus on the real reason we were there. She was going to help us, I was sure of it. Just keep moving forward.

There was just enough time for us to walk around the camp before the vigil was scheduled to begin. We decided to use the chocolate bars as a bargaining chip, a way to speak with people and tell them about the prayer vigil. Our goal was to get as many refugees assembled as possible. I would then sing the "Prayer of St. Francis" and at the same time millions of people would be sending their light. We picked what seemed like an appropriate place, and then I tilted my head back and looked toward the sky. One cannot see prayers that are focused in a certain way, at least not with the eyes. I knew that, and yet I also knew that they were on the way. I began preparing my mind for that moment.

It was very much like the Emissary wheel, I thought to myself, only I was the one in the center this time. It was my job to focus the prayers that fell upon us from around the planet. I had the same feeling as in Iraq, Northern Ireland, Israel, and during the Great Experiment — every time one of these vigils was held. I was used to it by then, an incredible sensation much like standing beneath a waterfall. I would feel the energy fall in and around me like waves of light, then I would focus that light, much like a child holding a magnifying glass to turn the scattered rays of the sun into a narrow laser-like beam of light. This was where the magic would happen, and I knew it. It certainly had nothing to do with me, at least not with me as an ego. I had to put my own motivations far away, as if I was just an instrument held in the hands of God. In this case it was Maria that was holding me, and I could feel her touch just like I had on the hill in Medjugorje.

I gave Gillian half of the chocolate bars and we decided to go in different directions. In this way we would be able to talk to more people, let them know what was about to happen. We would meet at the designated spot twenty minutes before the vigil began. Hopefully by then hundreds or even thousands of people would be on their way. Then we would begin.

I stopped and looked around to get my bearings. There were thousands of tents lined in dozens of neat rows, and in front of several large tents hundreds of people were lined up waiting for something I could not immediately determine. I walked up to one of the lines and found a man who spoke English.

"This line is for Germany," he said. "Every line you see is for a different country, and we get into the line of the country we want to go to."

"So you want to move to Germany until the war is over. What happens then? Do you want to return to your home?"

"Of course, but we do not know how long that will be. It could be a very long time. We are very happy NATO has come to help us, but we cannot stay here in these tents. We must leave here, then return when it is safe."

I walked around the camp, overwhelmed by the sights and sounds that overcame my senses. Everywhere I looked, I could see small red balls flying through the air, with children, adults and even soldiers kicking them on dozens of make-shift soccer fields. Then I saw old people sitting in front of their tents without moving at all, holding very still as if they were statues. I looked at one such woman and had the sensation that she wasn't there at all. I saw tears and I heard laughter, people who appeared broken in two and others who were still whole. It was so multi-dimensional that I couldn't really pinpoint anything, or anyone. It was not at all as I expected.

As I walked along the dirt road that separated two long rows of tents I felt a strange sensation, one that I was learning to instantly recognize. It was her, Maria, and I could feel her presence somewhere nearby. My mind was suddenly overwhelmed, and yet I couldn't be sure if my instincts were correct. The idea itself was completely satisfying, and it soothed a part of me that was hurting for these people. But what if she really was there, I thought to myself? Perhaps she was the reason we had soared through every possible obstacle and arrived at the camp so easily. Maybe I was about to see her again, the Beloved that made my heart sing.

I began walking faster and faster as if my legs alone could bring me straight to her side. My eyes darted back and forth, watching for a sign, any faint image that would lead me to her. Once or twice I thought I saw her, and I ran to have a closer look. But each time it turned out to be a young blonde Kosovo girl, and I went on searching.

Maria, if you're here, please show yourself. I need you. I've always needed you. Show me what to do in this sad place. Show me how to be truly helpful. Use me to touch these people and bring them some comfort. I can feel you as if you're right beside me. If you are, if you're really here, then let me know somehow.

Just then I glanced toward one of the tents and saw an old woman crawling out on her hands and knees. Our eyes connected just as she sat up, positioning herself next to a small baby sleeping on a pile of blankets. She smiled and motioned for me to come over to her. Hesitantly I walked in her direction and stopped a few feet from her side.

"Are you looking for me?" she asked in English.

"I don't think so," I said to her. "I'm just walking..."

"Are you looking for me?" she asked again.

There was a gleam in her eye that was familiar, and when I looked past the outer mask I could feel an unfathomable depth. It was her. It was not an old woman at all. It was Maria, the Beloved.

"Yes, I am looking for you. But how can you be…"

"Remember what I said to you," she said. "When you first saw me in Belgrade, how did I appear?"

"As a student?"

"As an ordinary student, and you didn't recognize me. Then on the hill in Medjugorje I explained the essence of my whole teaching. Do you remember what it was?"

"Yes. You said to find the Divine in everyone, in the ordinary."

"That's right," she said with a toothless smile. "Look past the appearance and see my face in everyone, at all times."

Suddenly the woman's eyes changed and she looked at me strangely. She began to speak to me, but not in English. Maria was gone, and the old woman had returned. I held out a chocolate bar, then stood up to leave.

"Where are you going?" a middle aged man said as I passed him. "Walk with me for a moment."

I looked into his eyes and was utterly amazed. They were her eyes, the same glowing orbs of light I had seen many times before. She was actually bouncing from one person to another, and in doing so was teaching me the most essential lesson of all.

"There is only one real gift you can give them," he said. "The food you bring will feed only their bodies, but if you are willing to look deeper, past the masks and egos, then you will perceive the truth in them. That is when you will truly be of service, for that's what they want most of all. Look at this body in front of you now. It is tired and rugged, exhausted from days and weeks of trying to stay alive. You can give him one of your chocolate bars if you want, but it will not solve the real problem. But if you look to the truth in him, the essence where I am right now, then a spark will come alive that has the power to transform his life. You can do that simply by looking past all the ways he seems different and separate from you. Focus on the ways you are the same, and that sameness will take you to the soul where all reality is one."

Once again the look was gone and the man stared at me strangely, as if he had just woken up from a dream. I smiled at him, then turned away, wondering where she went.

"Over here," I heard a voice say. I saw a small girl sitting alone next to a tent, smiling at me. I walked over and sat down at her side.

"Maria, is that you?"

"I'm whoever you want me to be," she said. "Even your definition of Maria is a limitation. You need to let go of even that and embrace the formless reality that is just beyond all appearances. You think that Maria is different from Jimmy, or this little girl. There is no Maria, and there is no Jimmy. There is only the Divine. There is only Light. The world is a game, but you can't enjoy the game until you realize that. Even here, in this desperate place, you are challenged to look past everything and see the truth.

"Do you really want to be an Emissary of Light?" she continued. "Well this is how it happens: Let go of every idea of who you think I am, who you think God is, and who you think you are. Let it all go, and see the world through the eyes of God, the eyes that see everyone as the same, blanketed in holiness and grace. Then you will understand what it really means to be an Emissary. Then you'll assume your own role as a Teacher of God."

"Maria, I understand what you're saying, but I'm still so far away. I still need your help to do these things."

"You don't need my help," said a young woman who walked up to my side. I stood up from the child and looked at her. "Look into my eyes," she continued. "What do you see?"

"I see two eyes, brown…"

"Look deeper, look past the physical eyes to the truth. Look at the Face behind the face, the Light behind all lights."

I felt my gaze soften and my focus deepen. Her eyes seemed to glow, and just for an instant I was no longer standing there next to the tent, or in front of a young woman. I could see the Door of Eternity. It was the same Door that Teacher had shown me the last time I ever saw him, the Door that leads to the real world. I was afraid of it then, but now it was calling me forward, pulling me in with such power that I could not resist. The Light seemed to envelop me, and I felt the most fantastic sense of freedom and joy. I can never describe what it was like, but in that moment everything made sense, and I understood everything.

"You're feeling Heaven," she said to me. "You don't need to die to feel the truth pulse through your veins. You just need to release your fear, then enter the Door of Eternity through the person right in front of you. I am always there… God is always there. You just need to be willing to look, and then you will see the only face there is to see — the face of the Divine."

"It's so simple, and so real," I was able to say. "How could I have missed this before?"

"Because you were afraid to look. Don't ever be afraid again, Jimmy. Everything is about to change, and you need to be ready for those changes. How else can you complete your mission?"

"What is my mission?" I asked her.

"You will see," she said. "It's not over yet, in fact it has only just begun. I can never leave you… you only need to look into another's eyes and you will see me again. Keep moving forward, and tell everyone to keep moving toward the Light. Humanity stands at the brink of reality itself. This is the time you've been waiting for. This is the moment when you wake up to the truth. Thank God for this chance, for you have journeyed a great distance to be here."

The young woman's face suddenly changed and I knew Maria was gone. But was she really? I smiled at her and she smiled back at me. It was a real smile, not put on or condescending. I reached into my pocket and pulled out a chocolate bar, then held it out to her.

I met Gillian an hour later. We had told as many people as we could about the prayer vigil and hopefully they would begin to arrive soon. Momentum was building, the feeling that Maria was still very present, the fact that millions of people around the world would soon be praying with us… it all seemed to be moving toward an outcome none of us could discern. Peace is like that, I realized. I had thought I knew a thing or two about peace, what it was and how it is achieved. But from the time I first met the Emissaries until I was standing there in the refugee camp, I realized I didn't know much at all… it was about unlearning everything I thought I knew. And there we were, thousands of miles from my home with tens of thousands of people who didn't understand what had just happened to them. We were very much the same, though our circumstances were dramatically different. The prayer we would share would be for us all, and the whole world would benefit from it.

I looked over at the mountains that separate Kosovo from Macedonia and saw the first strike of lightning flash from the dark ominous clouds. They seemed to be moving in our direction, and I noticed many of the refugees heading back to their tents. Within minutes the rain began to fall, and the long lines of people that had been standing outside sought shelter beneath the huge white processing tents. The ground turned to mud and the sky suddenly opened, flooding the makeshift roads and narrow paths. An Italian soldier motioned for us to come with him to a nearby tent hospital where we could keep dry. Gillian and I wondered what we would do. The vigil would begin in ten minutes, and the chance of the rain stopping by then seemed impossible.

We stood there in the makeshift hospital waiting — hoping the rain would stop. How could we have come so far and yet not achieve our goal? Against all odds we had been able to make our way to Skopje, then gain admittance to the camp. Millions of people around the world would stop what they were doing to pray, thinking that I was with the refugees. I was with them, and yet I wasn't. Tens of thousands of them were huddled together in tents trying to keep dry, and I was just like them, surrounded by Italian soldiers.

A Russian journalist was standing with us, another victim of the sudden downpour. He asked who I was with, or which press agency I represented. I tried to explain what we were doing, why we were there, but at that moment it sounded crazy, even to me. He couldn't understand why we wanted to travel this far to pray. "Why didn't you stay where you were?" he asked. "It seems strange that you would be here now, in this situation."

I was nearly ready to agree with him when an Italian officer stepped up to me. "You say you are here to pray...yes?" I told him why we had come to Macedonia, and all about our previous experience with mass prayer vigils. He listened intently, as if he was sincerely interested. Then he stepped away from us and spoke quietly to another officer.

"We have an idea," he said when he returned a moment later. "Why don't you pray with us? We can arrange to have many soldiers here and we will join all the people around the world who are praying at the same time. We can set up an area over there in the corner and you can sing your peace prayers as well. What do you think?"

It was a brilliant idea, one that I had not considered. Over and over I was learning the most valuable lesson — surrender. I didn't know what needed to happen, that was obvious. It was but mine to step back, and let it occur on its own. Every time I stepped back and let go of my own ideas, a miracle happened. That moment, in the hospital tent with the Italian soldiers, was no exception.

Moments later the tent was filled with soldiers standing side by side in the hospital. The rain hit the slanted roof of the tent and the thunder made for a dramatic overture. Some of the soldiers took off their hats in respect. Others spoke softly so as not to intrude upon the sacredness of the moment. I looked at my watch — one minute to go. The energy was beginning to build, and I looked over at Gillian. "Are you ready?" I asked her. She nodded her head.

"Bongiorno," I said to them. "Grazie. Thank you for taking time to be with us. In about a minute millions of people around the world will stop what they're doing to hold the people of Kosovo, as well as Serbia, in their hearts. You're all here in this camp because the international community refuses to watch this tragedy happen, and they are not going to let Serbia succeed in its plan. But we're evolving, I believe, to a place where we won't have to use violence to end violence. That's why we gather here together in prayer, to assure the arrival of that day. It will come when we want it to come, when we realize that only love can vanquish fear."

I picked up my guitar and began to play the "Prayer of St. Francis." Even the soldiers who didn't speak English seemed to know the words. Several years earlier I had learned the prayer in Italian, but I could only remember one line: "O Signore, fa da me uno strumento della tua pace." I sang that one line over and over till they picked up the melody and joined me. As they sang I could feel the prayers of millions of other people from around the world flooding the whole region. They were there with us, as were all the refugees and the aid workers who were huddled in tents around the compound. And Maria was there as well, I was sure of it. I could feel her arms enfold us and envelop us in her love.

The prayers fell like rain, and we were drenched by the holiness of the moment. Then the rain stopped and the refugees began to leave their tents, flooding into the common areas and dirt roads. The soccer balls came with them, and they returned to their games. Gillian and I looked around in disbelief.

We had done it, whatever it was.

he is here, all around us, watching over us as a Mother. This is the chosen time for the release of Her Divine Light, the radiance of the "Feminine, Compassionate Nature of God." But she cannot do it without our help. We are the instruments through which this light is revealed. We are the vehicles that bring a New World into focus, one that is ruled by the reality of love, not the shadow of fear. We have lived in that shadow for too long. The Mother comes to us now with extended hands, ready to lead us into the Light. Will we take her hand, or continue to cower in the corner of our darkened minds, afraid to look into the face of love?

As I look back over the last few years I am amazed and overjoyed at how blessed my life has been. I made a promise to Maria when I was a child, and no matter what I did, no matter how I tried to extinguish the Light within me, she would not let me forget. She waited patiently in the background, waiting for the right moment to reveal herself to me again. And how could I have prepared myself for that glorious coming? How could I have known she would reveal herself to me so directly, in a way that was completely ordinary, and yet wholly Divine? I was finally ready, I guess. And that was her whole message, and the Emissary's message before her. We are all ready for this New World, whether we realize it or not. That was what she came to reveal to us all. And as I continue to travel around the world singing the prayers of peace, I realize she is right.

How simple is salvation. Those are the words that continually echo in my ears. It's time to stop trying to complicate what needs no complication. The Door of Eternity is always open; we just have to look into the eyes of whoever is right in front of us to see it. And when we see her in their eyes, the Radiant Light of the Divine, then we are pulled into Heaven without effort. Heaven requires no effort at all, just a little willingness. We just have to ask for help, then trust what we're shown — the vision of a healed world. That world is waiting to be revealed through us, through our own desire and commitment to the truth. And what is the truth? It is that you are already healed, already whole and already enlightened. Maria's job is just to remind us of those facts.

Where do we go from here? We travel to the home we never left, the Kingdom we never squandered, except in our imagination. That will also manifest in the world we live in. How could it not? The world is nothing more than the extension of our thoughts about ourselves, each other, and God. When we change those thoughts, choosing to perceive holiness instead of attack, love instead of fear, then the world must change as well. That's just how it works. The world will reflect the grace that has set us free. This is indeed a glorious time to be alive — perhaps the best of times.

Several weeks before the Serbian Army pulled out of Kosovo and NATO troops moved in to enforce the cease-fire, Fr. John faxed a letter to Archdeacon Radomir Radic, the assistant to the Serbian Orthodox Patriarch, whom he had met on a previous journey to Belgrade. Months earlier John had showed up at the Archdeacon's office unannounced and asked if they could pray that the spiritual victory promised to Tzar Lazar should finally be realized. The Archdeacon told his secretary to hold all calls, and together they knelt in the office and prayed for at least half an hour. Months later Fr. John faxed his friend a letter, a portion of which I have included here:

My dear brother in Christ,

It was barely a year ago at this time that I visited you in Belgrade. After we talked for awhile about things political and spiritual, as well as our shared Christian values and our love for what had been Yugoslavia, I remember that right there in the middle of your very busy day you told your secretary to hold your calls, locked the door, and then we got down on our knees and prayed for the healing of the soul of your great nation, and that Serbia might fulfill her true spiritual destiny.

I have thought often about our visit and our prayer time together since then, especially with the events of the past five months and now with the NATO bombings. Some one million people in Kosovo have been driven out of their homes and their country. In turn, the bombings have now reached such a point that in addition to the terrible damage inflicted on the infrastructure of your country and the many innocents that have been killed, the spirit of the earth herself has become so wounded and offended that she is ready to rise up in wrath. Truly something terrible for your country and the whole world will happen if the bombing and the war do not stop. And yet it goes on.

We are very close to reaching the point from beyond which there will be no possibility of return or turning back. I sense that a Divine Intervention is near. And it is not to be one of wrathful judgment and complete catastrophe; there will have to be an intervention of prayer, and it will have to come from within Serbia. Indeed, that is precisely what has come to me in my own prayers — a true resolution of all this can only come from within your own country. And that is why I am writing to you, my dear brother in Christ. I know that you are a man of the same God as I am, devoted to the same Holy Mother as I am, and the servant of the same Christ and his commandments. Only a spiritual intervention can solve this and it must come from and through the Church and the faithful in Serbia. My prayers and those of millions of others are with you, but only you can act.

So I beg you, in the name of the Holy Mother, to intercede with the Patriarch and ask him to demand that Milosevic submit to the authority of Mother Church and repent and convert. Remind him that Tzar Lazar of blessed memory, when given the choice by our most Holy Mother of the material victory and the earthly kingdom, or the spiritual victory and the Heavenly Kingdom, chose the spiritual victory and the Heavenly Kingdom. And to attain that victory and its fruits for those who would come after, sacrificed his own life and that of many of his warriors. Milosevic has however made the opposite choice.

In choosing instead the material victory and the earthly kingdom, and attempting to reverse the Battle of Kosovo [held at the Field of the Blackbirds over six hundred years ago], driving out the Muslims who have lived there since then... Milosevic has gone directly against Tsar Lazar, insulting his memory and sacrifice, and is now bringing about its physical destruction.

Only the Church and the Church's spiritual authority can save the integrity of your country, and by her intervention, call the people to return to the faith and its practice. By now many of the people in your country are sick to death of all this, but have no way of turning on Milosevic without seeming to support NATO. You however are in the position to provide a Serbian alternative coming from within Serbia, having true and right spiritual authority.

Please pardon my boldness in addressing you and the Patriarch so, but God has asked it of me. This is the word and vision that God has given me to give to you. Please pray yourself to see that it is of Christ and the most Holy Mother, then make it your own and present it to the Patriarch. I am totally at your and your country's service as I know her spiritual destiny is at stake and hangs in the balance now, and the significance this has for the world.

With all love and blessings and respect,
Yours in Christ's service,
Fr. John
Community of the Beloved Disciple

John called this his flaming arrow. He faxed me the letter and I filed it away, sure that it would be of some significance later.

A week after the Serbian withdrawal I was reading the New York Times and came across an amazing article. The Patriarch had just issued an official statement calling for the immediate resignation of President Milosevic. Maybe John's flaming arrow got through, I thought to myself. As I read the article, as well as a portion of the actual statement made by the Patriarch, I thought about my friend. How would the Patriarch's summons serve the awakening of the New World, the Divine Feminine, and the re-emergence of the Community of the Beloved Disciple?

Then I went to my desk and found the letter John had sent to the Archdeacon. There it was, John's letter, almost identical to the statement in the newspaper. They had actually borrowed some of his words, his sentiment, his longing for healing and destiny.

Maybe the Emissaries really are right, I thought to myself. Maybe we are ready.

In Conclusion

wonder how she will use these things to continue her mission, that of helping humanity enter into the experience predestined since the beginning of time. I'm still not exactly sure who 'she' is. Is she the Mary I was raised to love, the Blessed Mother I was told cherished and watched over me, or is even that title a limitation? Perhaps she is that and more, so filled with Light that she is the new prototype for us to follow into the next millennium. She said that we had entered a new era, the era of compassion and grace, where love is the single reality and fear a forgotten dream. I believe she is right, and so were the Emissaries. I believe this is the time we've been waiting for.

Most important, we are all the Mother, and we are all giving birth to the same light. Maybe this is what was meant by the Second Coming all along. We have been looking outside, waiting for someone else to carry the torch. In reality, we are the only ones who can accept the Light and Peace of God. This new era, this great shift we have all heard so much about, has been about self-realization, about activating the reality within that has not forgotten the truth. We are ready... we are ready to accept ourselves for who we really are, rather than who we have never been.

Jacqueline, Fr. John and I had the same prayer, to be used as instruments of peace. I don't know how the painting and the music will move people, or how it will help us move into the New World which Maria spoke of, but I am overjoyed to have played a part, no matter how small. One thing I know is that she is still with me, just as she is with all of us, just as God never left us alone even for an instant. Maybe that's what has happened, we're finally able to realize that we're not alone. If that is the real moral of this story, it's the best news I've heard in a long time.

Well into the writing of this book I received a phone call from Fr. John who said that he and Shrinat Devi had to talk to me. They said it was very important. I was scheduled to do a concert near Los Angeles and set aside a few days to spend with them. John and I drove to Shrinat Devi's house, that familiar, holy place where I first learned of Maria, when her coming was first announced to me. It felt good to be with my friends again, and to share everything that had happened over the last few months. I had come full circle since that day when I first heard about the Emissaries. I finally knew who they were and where we are all going.

"Then you know what needs to happen next?" Shrinat Devi asked.

"I never really know," I told her. "But I believe we will all be shown. Maria has promised that."

"Shrinat Devi and I have been talking about the next step," John said. "This healing of Peter and John you spoke about... this is the direction where we need to be moving. There are too many people who have been injured by their past, especially by the dogmas and rules of many of the institutional churches. In many cases, because of these injuries, they have broken away from the churches they were raised in and have turned toward freer expressions of their spirituality. But they haven't been healed. They carry their resentment around with them and call themselves things like, 'recovering Catholic.' They are like adults who resent the way they were treated by their parents, but instead of forgiving their parents they never see them again, forgetting not only the trauma but the love as well."

"What they don't realize," Shrinat Devi continued, "is that they are now being called back to dance in the aisles of the churches that once injured them. There are so many people who have received profound gifts from spirit, and these gifts can help those who are still bound to more institutional forms...help them enter into a deeper relationship with God. That's how the ancient schism between Peter and John will be healed, through people like us opening to our past and returning to share our gifts. If we continue to guard our gifts and not share them, then we stop growing."

"And likewise, Peter has gifts to offer John," John said. "The wisdom of the ages is found in the esoteric traditions of every major religion. Once we move past the outer shell we come to the heart, and just as the heart of every person in the world beats the same, regardless of their race or creed, so does the inner wisdom of every religion resound with the same truth. As Peter and John come together to share their gifts and the wisdom they have each attained over thousands of years, the wall between the inner and the outer church, the esoteric and exoteric traditions, will crumble. This sounds like the real message of Maria, that it is time for us to come together, to focus on the ways we are the same rather than the ways we are different."

"And how will we do that?" I asked.

"You said that the Community of the Beloved Disciple held the essence of the Divine feminine for two thousand years, waiting for the masculine to run its course," Shrinat Devi said to me. "The time has now come for that energy to be revealed… to empower the religion of compassion and peace rather than conversion and domination. It will happen in many ways, since the Mother is giving the same message to many other people in the world. Each one of them will establish their own link to this light. But what happened to you is unique. There is a direct link between the Emissaries you encountered and the apostle himself. It is your job to reestablish the outer manifestation of that order which has been underground and hidden for a thousand years.

"The two of you, Fr. John and Jimmy, share the same mission," she continued. "John stands facing the hidden world, and Jimmy stands facing the physical world. You stand back to back, one pulling breath from the spiritual hierarchy and the other giving that breath to humanity itself. You have the same mission, though you will express it in different ways. And Jacqueline has played her role as well, a role no one else could have played. She answered the Mother's call and allowed the light to be made manifest on a simple painter's canvas. That canvas, along with the music the Mother inspired, will move people in ways that have yet to be revealed. Humanity is ready for this, and each one of us has a role to play in the new drama of life."

"We think you need to begin a mystery school based on everything that was revealed to you by the Emissaries and Maria," John said. "We'll help you. The 'New Emissaries' will emerge from that school, and the ancient order will be in the open again."

"But I wouldn't know how," I protested.

"You don't have to know how," Shrinat Devi said as she took my hand. "You are not in charge of this… She is. Those who are ready will come, and then they will go out into the world and heal the ancient schism between Peter and John. They will be brothers again — the inner and the outer. Then the world of duality itself will fall."

"The last thing I want to do is establish a new priesthood," I said. "That's one of the things that has caused so much confusion… that we need an intermediary between ourselves and God."

"In the Community of the Beloved Disciple we are all priests and priestesses, or at least we are equal" John said. "That was one of the reasons the Roman Church tried to destroy the different orders, because there was no hierarchy. Even the sacraments were shared by all. In the Catholic Church, for example, only a priest can consecrate the bread and the wine during mass. Through his power, it is believed, they are transformed into the body and blood of Jesus. The lineage of John had a different way of looking at this sacrament. They believed that everything is infused with the light of the Divine. In the Johannian mass we use whatever is in front of us, just as Jesus did during the Last Supper. He took bread and wine because they were in front of him. And so shall we take what is in front of us, and use it to express the Divine."

"And that brings us to the real thing we want to discuss with you," Shrinat Devi said. "It's time for you to be officially consecarted into the Order. The consecration is just an outer symbol of what you are already, but it will have value as you continue your work. John, who is a priest in both the Church of Peter and John, is the one to impart this blessing. You in turn will welcome others, all those who are called to enter the Community of the Beloved Disciple."

"And what will these others do?" I asked.

"They'll carry out the original mission of the Community," John said to me. "They will hold the Feminine energy of God in their hearts and they will extend that love to everyone in the universe. They will allow the Christ to be born in and through them, proving that Jesus did not die, for he lives within them. And they will help heal the ancient division between Peter and John, or the inner and the outer church. It doesn't matter if they are Christian or Jewish or anything else. This is not about religion, but about reality and love."

"You have been given an incredible gift," Shrinat Devi said. "Now it's time to share that gift. So the question is: are you willing to undergo this process... to take the vows of the Order?"

week later, at a chapel in Los Angeles, in front of Fr. John, Shrinat Devi and another friend, I said 'yes', and was officially accepted into the Order. The ceremony set into motion a range of experiences which I haven't even begun to understand, but which will certainly be revealed and shared as this journey continues.

Finally, on Easter of 1999, during a workshop I was leading in Glastonbury, England, around fifty people joined me in the ruins of Glastonbury Abbey. There, at the tomb of King Arthur, I celebrated my first mass as a member of the Community. We could feel the spirits of the ancient knights lean forward into the world of bodies and things, and we knew they were happy with what was happening there. They, in their own way, were also part of the Community of the Beloved Disciple. They too held and guarded the mysteries that are only now, after so long, being revealed to the world.

I cannot call myself a priest unless I recognize everyone in the same light. And so it is. We are all the access points, the bridges, and the Doors to Eternity that make clear the path to Heaven itself. The time of specialness has passed, and we find ourselves suddenly embraced by the realization that we are the same — holy beyond imagination.

As for the Community of the Beloved Disciple — Shrinat Devi is right. It is not up to me — but Her. This is Her mission, and we are all Her instruments of peace. It is ours but to step back and allow a new answer to be given to the world. And it has — we need but accept it. I believe that the Community of the Beloved Disciple will expand as it did two thousand years ago, and that all the mysteries it has held in secret will be finally understood and lived. I will do what I can to bring about whatever healing is required, but I will not cloud the issue. Whatever happens, whatever I do or do not do, it will be for the world which Maria has shown me. This is the time we have waited for.

Beloved CD

The CD mentioned in Part Three of this book can be purchased for US $15 (+$3 shipping and handling within the US or $5 outside the US). The CD features Jacqueline's painting "Our Lady of the Universe", a photograph of the miraculous candle, a rendition of Maria from the photograph taken on the hill in Medjugorje, as well as the music recorded by James Twyman at the Presidio Chapel in San Francisco. Please send check (US funds only please) to:

Beloved CD
P.O. Box 1786
New London
NH 03257
USA

The Reemergence of the Community of the Beloved Disciple

A formation study program has been started to initiate people into the Community of the Beloved Disciple. This six month program is run through the Internet and requires an email address. For more information, visit our website emissaryoflight.com or send an email to BELOVEDJT@aol.com requesting more information.

If you would like to be on our mailing list, please send a letter (including email address) and S.A.S.E. to:

Emissary of Light
P.O. Box 1786
New London
NH 03257
USA

FINDHORN Press

Findhorn Press is the publishing business of the Findhorn Community which has grown around the Findhorn Foundation in northern Scotland.

For further information about the Findhorn Foundation and the Findhorn Community, please contact:

Findhorn Foundation

The Visitors Centre
The Park, Findhorn IV36 3TY, Scotland, UK
tel 01309 690311 • fax 01309 691301
email reception@findhorn.org
www.findhorn.org

For a complete Findhorn Press catalogue, please contact:

Findhorn Press

The Park, Findhorn,   P. O. Box 13939
Forres IV36 3TY   Tallahassee
Scotland, UK   Florida 32317-3939, USA
Tel 01309 690582   Tel (850) 893 2920
freephone 0800-389 9395   toll-free 1-877-390-4425
Fax 01309 690036   Fax (850) 893 3442
e-mail info@findhornpress.com
findhornpress.com

New from Findhorn Press

Christ Power and the Earth Goddess: A Fifth Gospel

by Marko Pogacnik

ISBN 1-899171-92-4

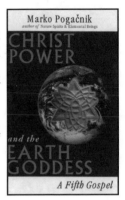

Romancing the Gospel...

Marko Pogavcnik has always been convinced that there existed a fifth Gospel, one that would be relevant for the challenges facing humanity as it enters the third millennium.

Here we have stories filled with the excitement of a detective book, where the author researches and investigates and travels to distant lands. Using his remarkable investigative powers, Pogacnik discovered this new Gospel composed of separate messages woven into the text of the canonical Gospels. These offer perspectives sharply different from the usual biblical interpretations. They speak of love and wholeness, male and female, and the union and communion of all humanity with the Earth and the realms of Angels. The dualism of good and evil has no part in them. Pogacnik concludes that the Fifth Gospel was edited out of the canonical texts, either because their message was too far removed from contemporary understanding, or because they interfered with plans for the formal, hierarchical theo-political structure which we know as the Church. Yet these lost messages of Jesus are deeply meaningful for our present time and our transition to the next stage of our evolution.

The choice is ours. We can move forward as one to a new plane of evolution, reconnect with the Christ Power that is in each one of us, and create a communion with our Planet Earth. Love, reconciliation and the consciousness of the heart will be our guiding stars in the coming days. In the words of Jesus himself, we can create Heaven on Earth.

> *Slovenian artist Marko Pogavcnik has an international reputation in conceptual and land art. Through his work he has developed the skill of Geomancy as a tool for unlocking the hidden wisdom of the Earth. He leads workshops throughout the world in Earth Healing and advises communities and businesses in landscape planning.*

New from Findhorn Press

The Celestial Voice of Diana:
Her Spiritual Guidance to Finding Love

by Rita Eide

ISBN 1-899171-03-7

"A rare account, filled with wisdom, clarity, love, and higher vision. Many important principles are brought to light in this inspiring text. One to be savored."

—Alan Cohen, author of *A Deep Breath of Life*

"I love this book with its message of universal love and truth and was fascinated by Diana's account of her mission from the spiritual dimensions, presenting a higher perspective of life. It is essential reading."

—Diana Cooper, author of *A Little Light on Ascension*

"This is an important, extraordinary book—comforting, inspiring, stimulating, confirming, frightening, but always relevant and resonant. I am hopeful that people will open their hearts and minds to its profound wisdom, and I am deeply grateful to Rita Eide for her work and to Diana for her love."

—Enid Futterman, author of *Bittersweet Journey*

"There is a beautiful vibration in this channelling which connects readers with the archetypal mother of the universe."

—William Bloom, author of *Money, Heart and Mind*

"For those who accept that "A Course in Miracles" originate from Jesus for the benefit of todays world and that "Conversations With God" originate from God, it should be easy to accept that this book actually is the "spiritual legacy" of Princess Diana. This is channeled material of exceptionally high standard."

—Roald Pettersen, editor of *Alternative Network*

New from Findhorn Press

Growing through Joy
by Ulla Sebastian

ISBN 1-899171-67-3

You want to grow. You want to expand your consciousness, become more powerful, more loving, more creative, more compassionate. But the last thing you want to do is go back through old memories, trying to resolve past agonies, suffering and tears in order to get there.

Here is the good news: you don't need to do that. There is a way to let the past go and choose an easier, far more natural way to achieve your goals. Growing through Joy!

Life is a choice. You can consciously move down the spiral of life into depression, stress, anxiety and pain. Or up into joy. Suffering has its attractions; we have had so much of it, we feel at home there. We have been told we have to struggle to achieve our ambitions. Who ever told you that life is always meant to be easy, joyful and fun?

Reading this book, and doing the easy exercises offered, may be the very best thing you have ever done in your life. And when you have found that essential joy in your life, when you find it bubbling over into all areas of your daily experience, share it with everyone around you. In fact, you won't be able to stop yourself, joy is contagious and irresistible.

Take a little time to learn the simple truths in these pages. It will be time well spent and will change your life.

Dr. Ulla Sebastian is a psychotherapist, workshop leader, trainer for Bioenergetic Analysis and practitioner of Holographic Repatterning. She was a member of the educational faculty of the Findhorn Foundation for ten years, and now lives in her native Germany, writing and giving lectures and workshops throughout Europe. She is the author of numerous books.

New from Findhorn Press

O Lanoo!
The Secret Doctrine Unveiled

by Harvey Tordoff

ISBN 1-899171-62-2

This book is addressed to you, the reader, seeker of truth, for Lanoo is the old Sanskrit word for spiritual student. It is an extra-ordinary story which starts before the creation of the universe. It tells of the time that gods lived on Earth, and how the Spirit of God came to live in Man. It follows the twin strands of evolution, in Spirit and in Matter, as the Ages of Lemuria and Atlantis gave way to our present Age.

O Lanoo! is a book for anyone on a spiritual path. It does not suggest a way of life or a new religion, nor does it offer life-enhancing techniques or meditations. Simply and eloquently it provides a complete picture of why we are here and who we are.

"An excellent book, that believe it or not takes on the challenge of writing the history of the world in the format of an epic poem, no less! Don't let that scare you — this is a gentle, loving book — inspired — I'd say. *Lanoo* means a student, a seeker of truth and if you're ready for an author to wrap his arms around you and take you on an inner universal journey, then you're ready for this one!"

—EAGLEeye, Spring 1999

"O Lanoo! is a powerful poem, a story in classic epic form, re-telling a hidden, Sanskrit text in rich and faithful style. *O Lanoo!* is based on the significant and weighty prior work of Helena Petrovna Blavatsky (the founder of Theosophy in 1875), whose work served author Harvey Tordoff well as he deftly brings this seminal, historical, and revered work to contemporary readers. *O Lanoo!* will prove to be greatly appreciated by all students of inspirational, New Age, and metaphysical studies. As a dedicated seeker of Truth, Tordoff has accomplished a masterful and important work for a whole new generation of the truth seekers."

—The Midwest Book Review